PENGUIN SELF-STARTER

# Typing

Gill Sugden has held full-time and temporary secretarial and administrative posts in the commercial and public sector in London and abroad. She is teacher-trained with a BA and MSc in Management Studies and has taught in the secondary, FE and HE sectors of education. At the present time she is subject leader in Office Communication Studies at the Polytechnic of Central London. Her lecturing includes keyboarding, word-processing and other applications software, and her particular interest is in the area of human factors associated with technology in the office. In the last few years she has been involved in developing syllabuses which reduce the teaching time for skills such as keyboarding to the minimum while still retaining a high standard in student achievement.

Alongside her work she has in the past marked typewriting scripts for public examinations and now works as a BTEC moderator and an external examiner. She undertakes some consultancy work that links directly with her lecturing interests.

SERIES EDITORS: Stephen Coote and Bryan Loughrey

# Typing

Gill Sugden

PENGUIN BOOKS

PENGUIN BOOKS

Published by the Penguin Group
27 Wrights Lane, London W8 5TZ, England
Viking Penguin Inc., 40 West 23rd Street, New York, New York 10010, USA
Penguin Books Australia Ltd, Ringwood, Victoria, Australia
Penguin Books Canada Ltd, 2801 John Street, Markham, Ontario, Canada L3R 1B4
Penguin Books (NZ) Ltd, 182–190 Wairau Road, Auckland 10, New Zealand

Penguin Books Ltd, Registered Offices: Harmondsworth, Middlesex, England

First published 1989
10 9 8 7 6 5 4 3 2 1



The figure on p. 95 is after N. Piercy ed., *The Management Implications of New Information Technology*, by kind permission of Croom Helm.

Filmset in Linotron Melior

Typeset, printed and bound in Great Britain by
Hazell Watson & Viney Limited
Member of BPCC plc
Aylesbury, Bucks, England

# Contents

# Introduction

This book is aimed at anyone who wants to learn to use a keyboard or improve on their existing knowledge. It is specifically geared towards the individual studying alone, but is also suitable for use by student groups aiming at keyboard mastery and a knowledge of business documents on a course with little time allocated to keyboarding skills. The book contains material which would enable someone who has worked through it to produce a range of documents commonly used in the office. The styles are suitable for typewritten or word processed work.

The content is broken down in the following way:

Readers can either begin at Chapter 1, which is an introduction to the keyboard for the complete beginner, or at Chapter 2, which covers the same material but from the point of view of the two-finger typist who wishes to improve keyboard knowledge, speed, or accuracy – or all three! Chapter 3 contains practice material which consolidates the lessons learnt so far.

The remaining chapters cover specific topics, for example the typing of letters, and explain the uses of different styles and document layout, with the help of typed specimens. Each of these chapters stands in its own right and can be used independently of the other chapters: cross-referencing ensures that all relevant information is easily accessible.

The second part of the book provides a variety of exercises for practice, many of which are in manuscript form. These are accompanied by keys, showing what the finished product should look like.

Having worked through the material covered in this book and achieved a reasonable standard of accuracy, readers would be able to enter for an elementary, and possibly an intermediate public examination in typewriting, should they wish to do so. However, they would need to ensure that they had reached the recommended speed for that examination.

## Keyboard plans

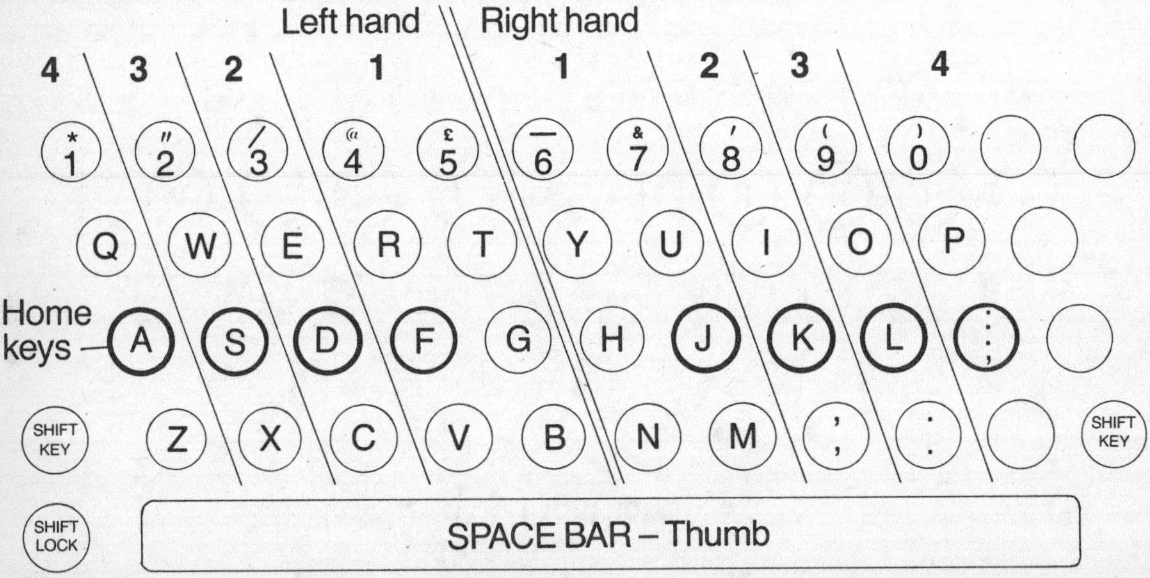


*Figure 0.1. Keyboard plan for those following Chapter 1.*

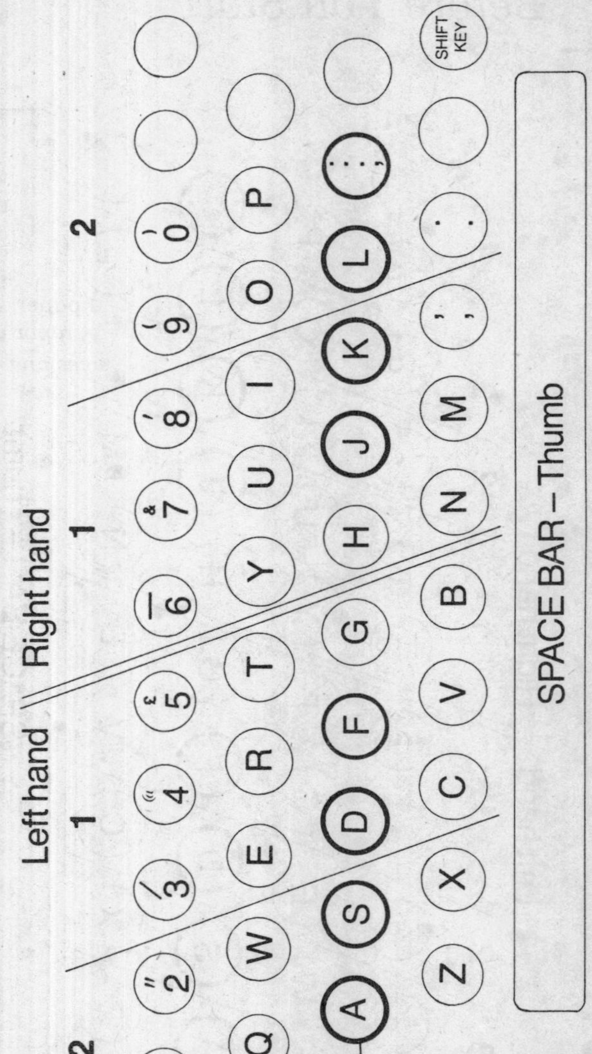


*Figure 0.2. Keyboard plan for those following Chapter 2.*

# Paper size and usage

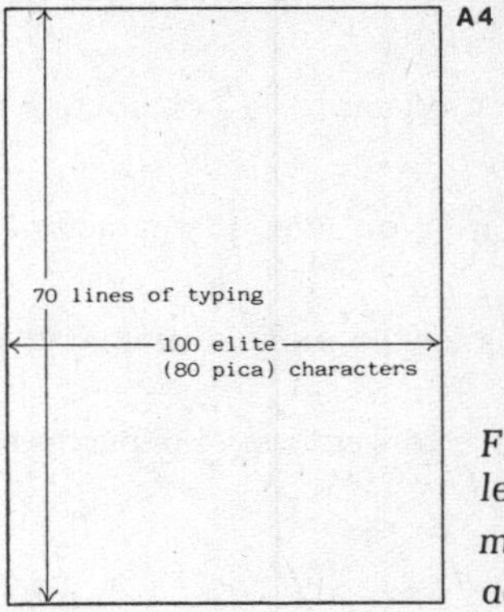


*Figure 0.3. A4 paper, used for letters, display, reports, minutes, invoices and accounts.*

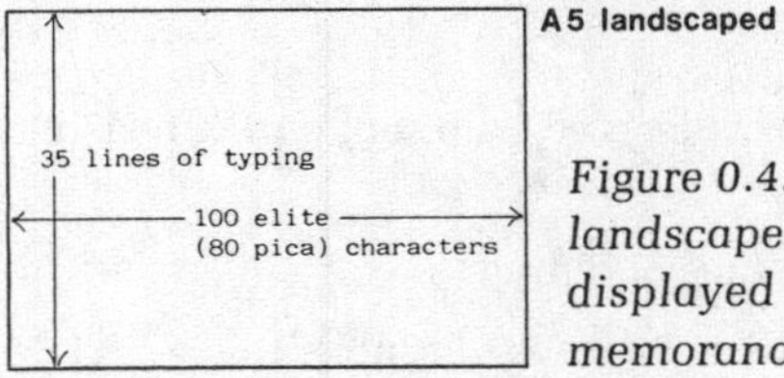


*Figure 0.4. A5 paper landscaped, used for displayed matter and memorandums.*

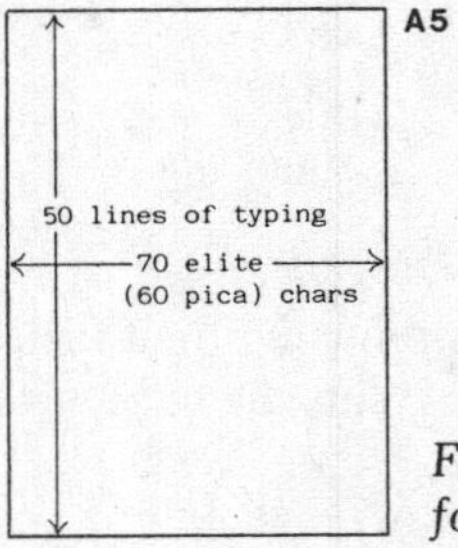


*Figure 0.5. A5 paper portrait, used for short letters and display.*

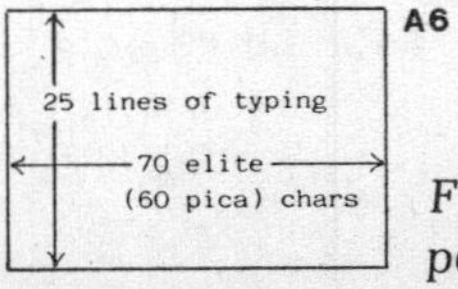


*Figure 0.6. A6 paper, used for postcards, invitations and itineraries.*

## Typing pitches

A machine with elite type gives 12 characters to 1 in or 25 mm

A machine with pica type gives 10 characters to 1 in or 25 mm

A machine with micro type gives 15 characters to 1 in or 25 mm

Refer to the previous diagrams for the number of characters across the various paper sizes.

Micro type will give 123 characters across A4 paper and 88 across A5 used portrait style.

## Lines to a page

The majority of typewriters give 6 lines of typing to 1 in or 25 mm. Therefore:

A4 has 70 lines of typing

A5 portrait has 50 lines of typing

A5 landscaped has 35 lines of typing

## Margin settings

It is practical to set the left-hand margin *wider* than the right-hand one. Business material is usually filed and the extra space allows the paper to be inserted in the file.

Suggested guidelines for margins are:

**A4**

1 in and 1 in (25/25 mm) = 12 and 88 elite (10 and 70 pica)

*or* 1½ in and 1 in (38/25 mm) = 18 and 88 elite (15 and 70 pica)

**A5 – landscape**
as A4

**A5 – portrait**
¾ in and ½ in (19/13 mm) = 9 and 64 elite (7 and 75 pica)
*or* 1 in and ½ in (25/13 mm) = 12 and 64 elite (20 and 75 pica)

(Pica margin settings will be given in brackets throughout the book.)

It is usual to estimate ½ in equal to 13 mm, 1 in equal to 25 mm and 1½ in equal to 38 mm.

# 1 The Keyboard

The aim of this chapter is to teach you to touch type. This means not looking at the keys so that you have your eyes free to look at the script from which you are copying. As the chapter proceeds you will also learn the use of many of the parts of the machine.

You cannot learn the whole keyboard satisfactorily in one day: it is better to assess how much time you can give to typing over a period of a few days. Then, divide the chapter up into comparable sections and do that much each day. When you begin on day 2, etc, quickly go through what you did on day 1 to refresh your memory, before beginning the new material.

It is important not to skip practice material that deals with parts of the machine because at some point, if you plan to type anything at all other than drills, you will need to be able to manipulate both paper and typewriter.

Each new point is numbered and headed for easy referral. However, it is impossible to give every variable for typewriter operation so it will be useful to keep the machine manual handy.

## 1 Getting ready to type

### *Suitable furniture*

Clear the table so that there is room for the machine, a light if necessary, and a book rest.

Try to use a chair that is adjustable for height and for the angle of the back. The back rest should support the lower spine, and the body should lean slightly forward from the hips. Sitting in a bad position and typing for any length of time can give you a very stiff back so it is worth spending a little time to get comfortable.

## 2 Parts of the typewriter

Use Figure 1.1 or the plan in your own typewriter manual to check that you can identify the parts of the typewriter. You will be using them all during the course of this chapter.

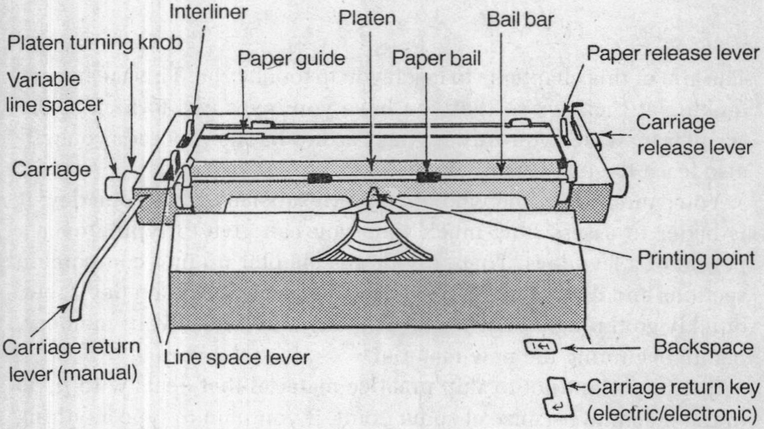


*Figure 1.1*

## 3 Inserting the paper

1. Slide the paper guide along to 0 on the paper guide scale as shown in Figure 1.2. Note that this lines up with the scale on the bail bar.

   If 0 is at the centre of the bail bar, as in Figure 1.3, the paper should be balanced on either side of the 0.
2. Use 2 sheets of A4 paper or a backing sheet (made of thin card) and a sheet of paper. This protects the platen or roller of the machine.
3. Hold the paper as shown in Figure 1.4 and slip it in front of the paper guide scale, with the left-hand edge against the paper guide.

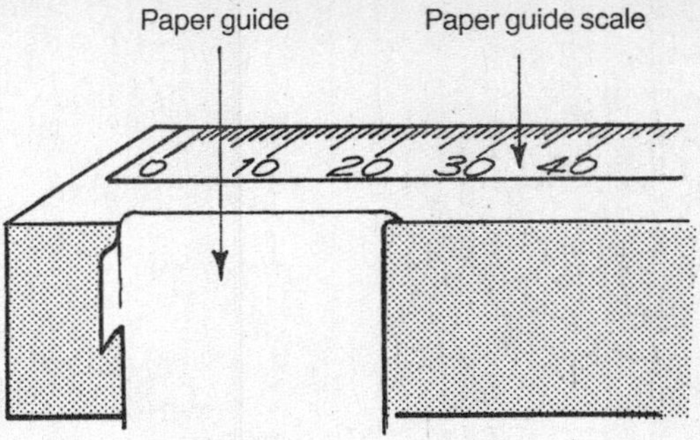


Figure 1.2

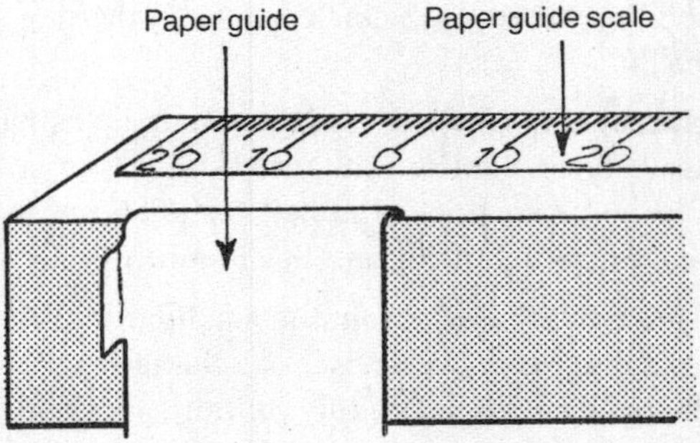


Figure 1.3

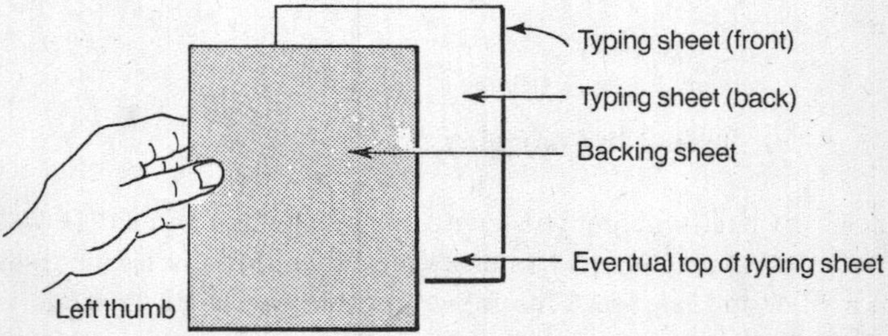


Figure 1.4

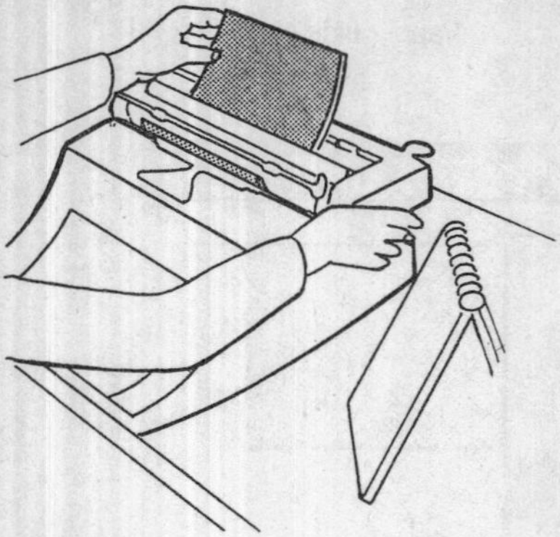

Figure 1.5

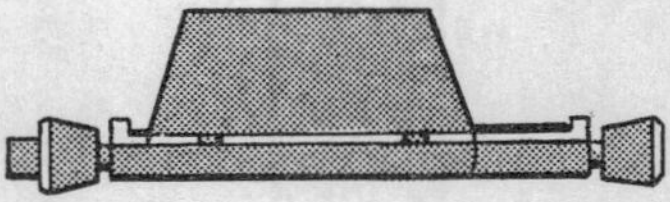

Figure 1.6

4. Turn the platen knob clockwise until the paper appears. (See Figure 1.5.)
5. If the paper is crooked, straighten it up by using the paper release lever. Return the lever to its home position and tuck the paper under the bail bar. The paper bails will keep it firmly in position. (See Figure 1.6.)
6. To remove the paper from the machine, continue turning the platen knob clockwise, or release it with the paper release lever. *Do not simply pull the paper out.*

Practise winding paper in and out of the machine several times. If you are using an electric or an electronic machine, there may be a separate control for inserting and removing the paper. Refer to your manual. Many of the above points also apply to printers used with word processors.

## 4 Setting the margins

Check whether you have a machine which types 12 (Elite) or 10 (Pica) characters to 1 in or 25 mm. If you do not know, then use a ruler to measure 5 ins from 0 on the paper guide scale. If 5 ins = 60 on the scale the machine is Elite and if 5 ins = 50 then the machine is Pica.

(On machines with a daisy wheel you can change the pitch simply by changing the daisy wheel so check what you have in the machine. The character of pitch type is printed on the wheel.)

Margins are usually set by sliding levers behind the paper guide scale. Initially set a left margin of 1 in or 25 mm. That is a setting of 12 on Elite and 10 on Pica. Set a right margin of 1 in or 25 mm, that is 88 or 70.

From here on margin settings will be given in Elite with Pica in brackets, thus: 12 and 88 (10 and 70).

If your machine has a different means of margin setting check with the manual.

## 5 Carriage return

To get from line to line in your typing you will need to use the carriage return; each time this is operated the typing point goes back to the left hand margin.

On a manual machine throw rather than push the carriage across with the flat of the left hand.

On an electric/electronic machine use the little finger of the right hand on the carriage return key.

Once the paper is inserted align the top edge with the scale on the card holder. Then return the carriage 7 times: this gives one clear inch at the top of the paper. The machine will use the 7th line to type the next set of characters.

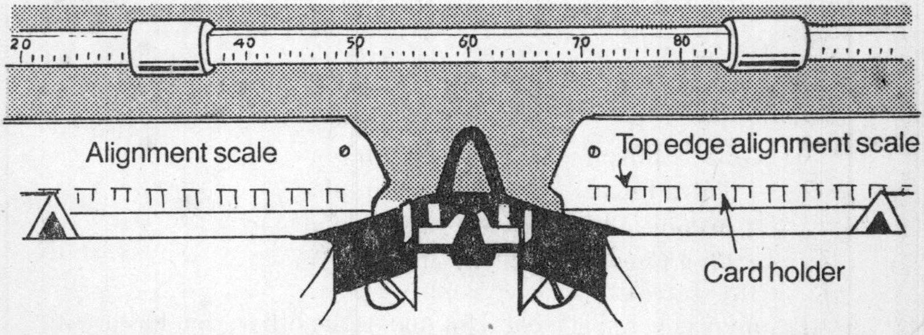


*Figure 1.7*

There are 6 lines of typing to 1 in or 25 mm on any standard machine. It is usual to leave 1 in clear on the top edge when using plain paper.

## 6 The alphabet keyboard

Tear out or photocopy the plan of the keyboard. You should be able to look at this as you work through the drills. Notice that the keys are not one under the other but slope down from the top-left corner towards the right.

The number above each section of keys indicates the finger to be used and which hand to use. *These never change!*

You should type the drills for each letter until you can complete them quite easily. *If you make a mistake, leave it. Do not overtype.* This is a bad habit to get into!

*Go at a speed which allows you to type evenly across the page.* Follow the line endings shown which means you will not be using the full width of the paper at first. It will be easier to remember the position of each key if you practise each drill.

### *The home keys*

With the left hand:

| | | |
|---|---|---|
| Little finger | **a** | (4) on plan |
| Third finger | **s** | (3) on plan |
| Second finger | **d** | (2) on plan |
| First finger | **f** | (1) on plan |

With the right hand:

| | | |
|---|---|---|
| Little finger | **;** | (4) on plan |
| Third finger | **l** | (3) on plan |
| Second finger | **k** | (2) on plan |
| First finger | **j** | (1) on plan |

Both thumbs cover space bar. Use one or the other, don't alternate.

Now you are ready to start. Feet flat on floor: body and head erect:

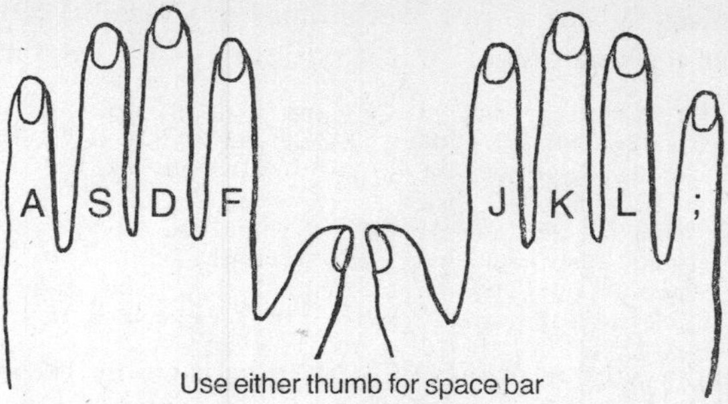


*Figure 1.8. This is the home position for your hands and you should aim to keep these keys covered as much as possible as you type.*

fingers lightly curved, hands flat across the back and wrists. *Wrists must not lean*. Eyes on the book.

Type the following (say each letter to yourself as you type it):

```
asdf ;lkj asdf ;lkj dafs k;jl dafs k;jl (carriage return)
as; da; fa; aa; la; ;ka ;ja f;a ja; df; (carriage return)
as add ass; lad; sad; dad; alas; salads (carriage return)
a; as all; lads asks lass; flasks fall;
```

All punctuation is followed by one space, except full stops which are followed by two. Try to type this space automatically as though it were part of the word it follows. If you do this you will always know where to begin typing again, rather than having to keep checking. When you are doing more difficult work you may sometimes need to stop and start.

```
a lad asks a dad; a lass asks a lad;
a dad falls; a sad salad; a flask falls;
```

### *Keys g and h*

With left hand:

**first** finger moves across from **f** to **g**

With right hand:

**first** finger moves across from **j** to **h**

Bring fingers back to rest over either **f** or **j**. Keep rest of hand in position over home keys.

```
fgf fgf fgf fgf jhj jhj jhj jhj fgf jhj
asdfgf ;lkjhj asdfgf ;lkjhj asdfgf ;lkjhj
a;sldkfjgh a;sldkfjgh ghfjdksla; ghfjdksla;

sad had dad hag gag all lag jag has ash
gash lash hash shag flag gall glad hall
sad flags; all shall flash; lash a gash;
a glad lass shall gash a flag; dad had a fag;
```

If you find a word or phrase difficult, practise it on its own.

On manual machines strike the key sharply. On electric and electronic keyboards slight pressure is enough to operate each key. Striking the key moves the carriage along one character.

### *Keys t and y*

Use **first** finger of left hand on **t**; **first** finger of right hand on **y**.

Remember to return to the home position. **Eyes on the book.** Feel your fingers reaching for the keys. *Don't look!*

```
ftf ftf jyj jyj ftf jyj ftf jyj ftf jyj
fgtf jhyh ftgf jyhj fgtf jhyj ftgf jyhj
fgft jhjy ftgf jyhj fgft jhjy ftgf jyhj
sat hat tag fat lay day hay gay say jay
that flat gaff hays stay says task slay
a lass had a sash; a flat tag; ask that
that lad stays flat; that hag has a gay hat;
```

This would be a good place to stop after the first day. To remove the paper use *paper release* lever, notice this brings the bail bar forward. (If you have an electronic machine look to see if there is another way of feeding the paper through and out of the machine.)

### *Keys r and u*

Use **first** finger of left hand on **r**; **first** finger of right hand on **u**.

Feet flat on floor: body and head erect: fingers lightly curved, hands flat across the backs and wrists. Eyes on the book.

```
frf juj frf juj frf juj frf juj frf juj
frtf juyj frtf juyj frtf juyj frtf juyj
ftrgf jyuhj ftrgf jyuhj ftrgf jyuhj
thy jug ray rut tug rat ark far jar art
```

```
dark thus tray hart glut lark hurt tart
drag lard lurk ruff husk full hard dusk
tally; shark; grassy; hussar; drake; lunar;
dad had a shark; a hart tugs at grass;
a guy hugs a lass; a dark lunar sky;
```

## Keys e and c

Use **second** finger of left hand on **e** and on **c**.

Remember to bring fingers back to cover home position on keys.

```
ded dcd ded dcd ded dcd ded dcd ded dcd
decd dced decd dced decd dced decd dced
car red cad jet cud the tea she use cut
sled flea flee lead ears duke cage cute
lease heart taste judge cheery dates flake
he used the ladder; she had a cheery red face;
the cat has a cage; the sea kale is as green as celery;
a lass frees the cats; dad tasted the tea as he ate the cake;
```

## Keys v and b

Use **first** finger of left hand on **v** and on **b**.

```
fvf fbf fvf fbf fvf fbf fvf fbf fvf fbf
fvbf fbvf fvbf fbvf fvbf fbvf fvbf fbvf
fvfgbf fvfgbf fvfgbf fvfgbf fvfgbf fvfb
vase vest ever have bald beat bees bush
brave saved every table shave valve sever
the lass served tea at the table; the heavy vats;
the lad had a brave try; they gave the lad a vest;
the bevelled glass cracked; the vast vat fell;
```

## Keys i and ,

Use **second** finger of right hand on **i** and on **,**.

```
kik k,k kik k,k kik k,k kik k,k kik k,k
ki,k k,ik ki,k k,ik ki,k ki,k ki,k k,ik
kit, mit, lit, bit, sit, fit, hit, git,
king, ring, sing, ming, sang, rang, tang, fang,
```

Remember, one space after a comma.

```
give me the tin, the can, and their bucket;
this car uses diesel, that one lead free gas;
the hotel is in the main street in the city, it is busy;
the sea is blue and there are many pale sails,
sit by me at the theatre this evening,
```

## *Capital letters*

Find the shift key on either side of the keyboard at the bottom. Using the fourth or little finger practise pressing it down. On a manual machine this is quite an effort at first.

To get a capital or upper case letter with a key that uses the left hand, press the right-hand shift key. The sequence is:

1. identify letter
2. press and hold shift key
3. strike required key
4. release shift key

To get a capital or upper case letter with a key using the right hand, press the left-hand shift key.

Now, type several times:

```
Aa Bb Cc Dd Ee Ff Gg Hh Ii Jj Kk Ll Mm Nn Rr Ss Tt Uu Vv Yy ;: ,,
```

(Your typewriter may have a slightly different keyboard layout for upper case, a question mark above the comma, for example.)

```
Andy, Beryl, Christine, David, Eric, Frances, Guelda, Hugh;
Ivy, Jasmin, Kenneth, Laura, Richard, Susan, Tracey, Ursula;
Violet, Yves:
```

## *Keys m and n*

Use **first** finger of right hand on **m** and **n**.

You will need to tuck your finger under for the m key.

```
jmj jnj jmj jnj jmj jnj jmj jnj jmj jnj
jmnj jnmj jmnj jnmj jmnj jnmj jmnj jnmj
jmjhnj jmjhnj jmjhnj jmjhnj jmjn
jam gun ram run hem hen ham hun van bun
lamb fine mast been mask vane mass limb
bank tank sank dank link kink sink mink
make a cake; taste the bun; rub the fat and sugar;
here are the lambs there are the sheep, that cage has ducks;
she has a jar of blackberry jam for the fine lad;
a jet needs fuel to fly; she had a black and blue scarf;
the lad buys fuel and then uses the car,
```

## *Keys o and .*

Use **third** finger of right hand on **o** and . .

You will find that your third fingers are weaker and you may need to go a little slower until you get used to using them all the time.

```
lol l.l lol l.l lol l.l lol l.l lol l.l
lo.l l.ol lo.l l.ol lo.l l.ol lo.l l.ol
old oat oil odd oak coy ton toe rod hog
tone boat vote roll mole coil gold gone
```

At the end of a sentence put 2 spaces after a full stop. Remember to think of it as part of the word you have just typed.

```
Rough. About. Brought. Touch. Shoulder.
```

Before typing the next phrases, check that your margins are set at 12 and 88 (10 and 70). (See page 12, Setting the margins.) Move the carriage, using the carriage release key, towards the right-hand margin. You should hear a bell when the typing point is 5 or 6 spaces from the margin. This warns you while you are typing that you are near the end of the line and you must either begin a new one or divide the next word. (Word division is discussed on page 48.) For now, you should use the margin release key to override the margin. This is usually placed on the left-hand side of the keyboard, and is marked ⇹. As you approach the margin, press it and it will release the margin for that line only, allowing you to complete the word.

```
The mole made a hole in the soil.  The man rolled the grass.
The tour of the town was boring.  In the morning I shall go
to the beach.  Today, I shall stay on the roof of the hotel
with them.
```

Try typing the above phrases several times. If you have a very uneven right margin try to improve on it at subsequent attempts.

## *Keys w and x*

Use **third** finger of left hand on **w** and on **x**.

```
sws sxs sws sxs sws sxs sws sxs sws sxs
swxs  sxws swxs sxws swxs sxws swxs sxws
wig wax saw six was way lax shy axe box
wind axle oxen west hoax brow flex when
```

Remember, leave 2 spaces after a full stop. Use your right-hand margin.

```
The bold judge wore a wig.  A waxwork figure was
found in the box.  When the west wind blows we shall
have bad weather on the brow of the hill.  Will you
wait for the saw and the axe.  The cows and oxen are
in the same field; what a mixture.
```

## *Keys p and ½*

(Your keyboard may have a symbol other than ½.)

Use **fourth** finger of right hand on **p** and on **½**.

```
;p; ;½; ;p; ;½; ;p; ;½; ;p; ;½; ;p; ;½; ;p; ;½p
;p½; ;½p; ;p½; ;½p; ;p½; ;½p; ;p½; ;½p; ;p½; ;½p;
l;p ;pl l;p ;pl l;p ;pl l;p ;pl l;p ;pl l;p ;pl
pay bap ply pin put pad ape rip tap pod
ripe pray path rope pine past prim wrap

Wrap the poppy in the wax paper.  Three ply wood was
made from ripe pine.  Please put your pins away.  The
cow, the pig and the ape shared a cage with the
porcupine.  Rather prickly.
```

## *Keys q and z*

Use **fourth** finger of left hand on **q** and **z**.

```
aqa aza aqa aza aqa aza aqa aza aqa aza
aqza azqa aqza azqa aqza azqa aqza azqa
quaint quickly queue quail queen queer quota
zoo zeal quiz size maze prize freeze zero
lazy zebra dizzy zest blaze zenith zest

We froze when the air reached zero.  Quickly, pass
him the special prize.  Zebras live in zoos.

Michael.  Neville.  Owen.  Penelope.  Queen. Walter.
Xavier.  Zenia.
```

Now you can type all 26 letters of the alphabet and you are ready to go on to learn the other keys and the numbers. But, if you think you need to do so, go back over any of the keys that give you trouble. Also, look at the following examples of common faults and see if any apply to you.

## 7 Diagnose your faults

**1.** `T yping is easy.  I 'm not so sure!`

When capital letters are above or below the typing line it means that you are not holding the shift key down while you strike the letter key. Check with page 18.

**2.** `Typing really is easy when you know how!`

You may be getting an uneven impression if you are using a manual machine; usually this happens with keys struck by the third and fourth fingers. Practise the relevant drills and also check that you are typing evenly. Ensure that you have an even rhythm and do not run together several letters you know well, only to hesitate before the next one.

If the full stop or other keys are making a heavy impression then try to strike the key a little less firmly. On an electric machine, if you are cutting holes in the paper try lightening the pressure. (Use your manual to find the adjustment which is usually a numbered dial or one marked – through to +.)

**3.** `I c an see I' m get ting better.`

There are 2 faults here. Firstly, you are not using the space bar correctly. It must be pressed sharply, not leant on – this will eliminate extra spaces between words. Secondly, by not striking the keys firmly and sharply but by being rather hesitant you can push the carriage along 2 characters rather than the 1 you want. If it occurs with particular letters then practise the drills for those letters again.

## 8 The numbers and upper-case symbols

You may find it hard to learn to touch type the numbers; this is because the finger reaches are quite long, especially on a manual typewriter. However, work through this part of the chapter to familiarize yourself with the position of the keys and particularly the upper case symbols.

Continue as before, type each line of drills several times: leave mistakes, do not overtype. Type the phrases and sentences until you can do them accurately.

Sit up: eyes on the book: feet flat on the floor: wrists straight, fingers slightly curved. Strike the keys sharply. Follow the line endings given for the short drills, make your own line endings for the sentences.

Hands covering the home keys.

## *Keys 4 5 6 7*

Use **first** finger of left hand on **4** and **5**. Use **first** finger of right hand on **6** and **7**.

```
fr4rf fgt5g fr4rf fgt5f fr4rf fgt5f fr4rf fgt5f
f4f f5f f4f f5f f4f f5f f4f f5f f4f f5f f4f f5f
ju7uj jhy6j ju7uj jhy6j ju7uj jhy6j ju7uj jhy6j
j7j j6j j7j j6j j7j j6j j7j j6j j7j j6j j7j j6j
```

```
The Arab had 4 wives.  One boy rode 7 bikes.  It is 54 miles
from London to Brighton.  There were 76 trombones leading
the big parade.  Fulham won by 5 goals to 4 at home and 6
goals to 4 away.  Please send 765 Christmas cards and 4
packets of tags.
```

## *Keys 3 and 8*

Use **second** finger of left hand on **3**. Use **second** finger of right hand on **8**.

```
de3ed ki8ik de3ed ki8ik de3ed ki8ik de3ed ki8ik
de3d ki8k de3d ki8k de3d ki8k de3d ki8k de3d ki8k
d3d k8k d3d k8k d3d k8k d3d k8k d3d k8k d3d k8k
```

```
Add 38 to 45 and you get 83.  The elephant herd consisted of 78
cows and only 3 calves.  The 8 men rang the 8 church bells.
There are 83 people on the beach, and 37 more are swimming.
```

## *Keys 2 and 9*

Use **third** finger of left hand on **2**. Use **third** finger of right hand on **9**.

```
sw2ws lo9ol sw2ws lo9ol sw2ws lo9ol sw2ws lo9ol
sw2s lo9l sw2s lo9l sw2s lo9l sw2s lo9l sw2s lo9l
s2s l9l s2s l9l s2s l9l s2s l9l s2s l9l s2s l9l
```

```
The 2 people made a pair.  There are 2 or 3 ways of doing the
job.  Take 22 from 99 and the answer is 77.  Add on 2 to make 79.
You need 2 or 4 players for a game of badminton.  Every cat has
9 lives.
```

## *Keys 1 and 0*

Use **fourth** finger of left hand on **1**. Use **fourth** finger of right hand on **0**.

If you have an older machine it may not have a figure 1. In that case use the letter l. However, you should not interchange 1 and l if you have both.

```
aq1qa ;p0p; aq1qa ;p0p; aq1qa ;p0p; aq1qa ;p0p;
aq1a ;p0; aq1a ;p0; aq1a ;p0; aq1a ;p0; aq1a ;p0;
a1a ;0; a1a ;0; a1a ;0; a1a ;0; a1a ;0; a1a ;0;

1 typed immediately before 0 gives 10.  Also 9 plus 1 makes 10.
0, 1, 3, 5, 7, 9, 2, 4, 6, 8.  72 added to 24 gives 96.  365 from
840 gives 475.  The 19th Century was from 1801 to 1899.
```

Remember use 1 or the letter l *not* capital I as this is used for Roman numerals.

The symbols above the numbers have specific uses which you probably know already. You can check them in Appendix 1.

The top row of the keyboard comprising the numbers and additional characters in upper case is fairly standard on modern machines. However, there are 4 other keys on the keyboard which have been left blank on the typewriter plan because the characters supplied and their actual position vary from manufacturer to manufacturer.

Remember to use the opposite shift key to the key you wish to strike, e.g. left shift key to strike &. The sequence is:

1. identify key
2. shift key down and hold with fourth finger
3. strike required key
4. release shift key

### *Keys £ and underscore*

```
f£f j_j f£f j_j f£f j_j
£27 £94 £395 £3.95 £6.00
```

Use the underscore sign to underline. If you have an electric or electronic machine, this will either be a repeater key which, if held down, continues to type across the page, or there will be a separate repeater key which can be used to the same effect with any key on the keyboard. On some electronic machines there is a switch or a code to put the machine on to the underlining mode. Follow the directions in your manual. Remember to turn the underlining off again!

To use the underscore on a manual or electric machine, first type the text, then use the carriage release to slide your carriage back to the beginning of the word or line that you want to underline. Many electric machines have a key marked ← for taking the carriage back along the same line. Now use the shift key and underscore. If you want to underscore a whole line, use the shift lock and then release it with the left-hand shift key. Everything typed while the shift key is down will appear in upper-case characters except on a computer keyboard.

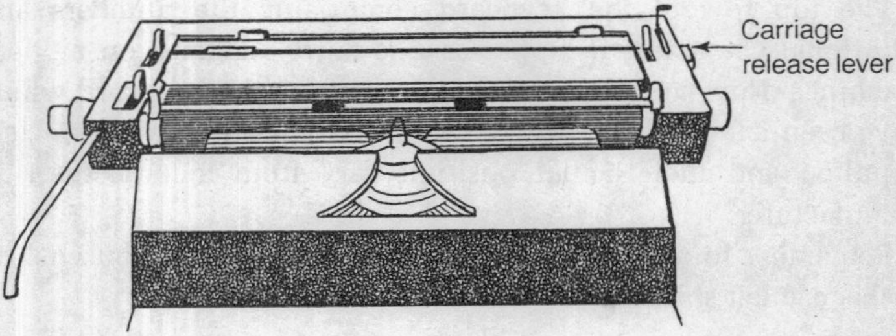


*Figure 1.9*

Use the Underscore sign to underline. The shift lock makes it easy to underline a lot of work. Underscoring should *not* extend under final punctuation:

Goodbye. ✓ Goodbye. ✗

## *Keys @ and &*

fr@f ju&j fr@f ju&j fr@f ju&j

I bought 6 pears @ 4p each. Envelopes @ 2p each cost 24p per dozen. Mr & Mrs Smith of 22 & 23 Kings Road. Messrs Rowell & Black. C W & J R Buchanan.

## *Keys / and '*

de/d ki'k de/d ki'k

3/4 1/2 7/8 1/4 2/3 Mr/Mrs/Miss/Ms It's already 6 o'clock, hasn't the day gone quickly. Isn't it time we went home, I'll get the car. It's John's car.

## *Keys " and ( and ?*

sw"s lo(l sw"s lo(l

The man said "Where am I?" The girl replied, "This town is in the centre of France". "Have a nice day." This time the man said "Who am I?" The girl said, "You are an Englishman on holiday. Don't you remember?" "No, I don't," he whispered.

## *Keys * and )*

aq*a ;P); aq*a ;p);

When you use the * sign it is automatically raised so that it is slightly above the line of typing (thus *). This means it is easy to use as a foot-note symbol.

Now type the following:

Please come and see me in my study (room 411).
Mr & Mrs Dransfield have renamed their home "Shalom" (formerly Cragside). My cousin was left £500 (five hundred pounds). The box measures 5½" x 4¼" x 3¾". The piece of wood was ½" x 24¼" x 8½".

To type an exclamation mark if your keyboard does not have one, use the full stop, *backspace*, and use the apostrophe symbol.

I've bought several dress lengths @ £2.50 and £5.00 each. What a bargain! Beware of the dog! That's mine! Go away!

See pages 21 and 49 for further information about upper-case characters and combination characters.

### *Hyphen*

Look for the hyphen on your machine. It is likely to be on the right-hand side of the keyboard and a lower-case character. Try to use the fourth finger to strike the key. Type the following:

```
We live in a self-contained flat over a self-service co-operative
store - it's so convenient!  Your car - a Mercedes-Benz is very
up-to-date - it has power-assisted steering.  Jane has bought a
house in a cul-de-sac.  I shall visit my mother-in-law on Sunday
- she has moved to Barrow-in-Furness.  Did you order the paper -
12 reams of A4 blue flimsy?
```

If you need to divide words use a natural break and do not change the pronunciation. For example chil-dren, not child-ren. It is better not to divide a word so that 2 letters are left at the beginning/end of a line. Some acceptable divisions for words would be pave-ment, neces-sary, con-sider, com-mitment, pass-ing, run-ning, under-stand, accommo-date. There is more information about word division on page 48.

The hyphen can also be used to give a dash in text. In this case a space is left before and after the hyphen sign.

If you are happy with the drills in this chapter you are ready to go on to Chapter 3.

# 2 The Two-Finger Typist

## 1 How to use this chapter

You may have used a typewriter for some time and either want to improve your typing or learn how to display work correctly. You could start right at the beginning of Chapter 1 and work through as if you were a complete beginner. You could go on to work through the chapters which meet your needs. Alternatively, you can try this chapter.

The aim is to make you familiar with the a–z on the keyboard, using the first and second fingers of each hand, and your thumb. Since you have probably already formed the habit of looking at the keyboard, the aim of this chapter is not to stop you from doing so, but simply to make you more familiar with the positions of the keys. In spending less time looking for them, you should be able to increase your speed.

You may find that in some cases it is easier for you to use a finger other than the one shown. If so, use it! However, it would be better to follow the system given, since it provides you with a firm basis of knowledge and movement for just over half of the alphabet. Try not to end up crossing your hands, since this will result in lots of errors!

Before you start you should read sections 1–5 of Chapter 1.

## 2 The keyboard

Now look at the keyboard plan on page 4. The keyboard has been divided into 2 halves. The keys will be introduced to you from the centre working outwards. You should try to keep your hands covering the home keys which are marked in black, because you will therefore have a base to work from. At the least keep the f key covered with the first finger of the left hand and j covered with the first finger of the right hand. Put both thumbs on the space bar and use the one that is easiest for you, but try to keep to using the one you decide is best for you.

Now, sit up: eyes on the book, feet on the floor, wrists straight with slightly bent fingers. Strike the keys sharply and follow the line endings as given. Say each letter to yourself as you type it.

### *Keys f g j h*

Use **first** finger of left hand on **f** and **g**. Use **first** finger of right hand on **j** and **h**.

If you can, try to feel your way to the keys rather than keep your eyes on the keyboard.

```
fgf jhj fgf jhj fgf jhj fgf jhj fgf jhj
fjgh fjgh fjgh fjgh fjgh fjgh fjgh fjgh
fhgj jghf fhgj jghf fhgj jghf fhgj jghf
```

### *Keys r t u y*

Use **first** finger of left hand on **r** and **t**. Use **first** finger of right hand on **u** and **y**.

```
frf ftf frf ftf frf ftf frf ftf frf ftf
juj jyj juj jyj juj jyj juj jyj juj jyj
frtgf frtgf frtgf frtgf frtgf frtgf frtgf
juyhj juyhj juyhj juyhj juyhj juyhj juyhj

fry guy hug jug tug rut thy try
```

### *Keys d and e*

Use **first** finger of left on **d** and **e**.

```
ded ded ded ded ded ded ded ded ded ded
derf derf edfg edfg ertg ertg derf derf

get jet red fed guy dye
fury tyre ruff guru jury grey
```

### *Keys s and a*

Use **second** finger of left hand on **s** and **a**.

```
fdsa fasd fsad fads fdsa fasd fsad fads

sad gas gay has ray ash
thus sued gust hart fade jars fuse feud jude fear

a sad hart a gay day
try the gas he has a fag
```

## *Keys k and i*

Use **first** finger of right hand on **k** and **i**.

```
kik kik kik kik kik kik kik kik kik kik
kiuk ikjh iuyh kiuk ikjh iuyh kiuk ikjh iuyh

did dig jig fig aid sky
duke saki rake take dyke kite hike fire
shake fudge sherry fairy ferry

the duke has a ferry ride
a great fire is lit in the grate
there is a green kite
```

## *Keys l and ;*

Use **second** finger of right hand on **l** and **;** .

```
jkl; j;kl j;lk jlk; jkl; j;kl j;lk jlk;
lad; ill; lid; kid; lad; ill; lid; kid;
kill sail ale; fall lass salt kill sail
```

After all punctuation except a full stop put one space.

```
shake the sails; kiss a lass;
dad had a hike; a high hill; the last day;
```

## *Keys w and o*

Use **second** finger of left hand on **w**. Use **second** finger of right hand on **o**.

```
sws lol sws lol sws lol sws lol sws lol
sweds loikl sweds loikl sweds loikl
was saw sew awe awl low owl ewe

slow wool stew lose wall oast
the wall was high; out of the road;
dry his shirt; wet her hair;
where is your foot; look at the hedge;
```

### *Keys q and p*

Use **second** finger of left hand on **q**. Use **second** finger of right hand on **p**.

```
aqa qsa ;p; pl; aqa qsa ;p; pl;

quite quiet quote quota quaver quiver quest
plait plate paste postal pride parade plaque

the wool was sent by post; it will look good;
take a quiet road today; where shall we go;
sail away to sea; sit quietly; hold tight;
```

Don't go any further than this in one day. You will not remember the sequence of the letters on the keyboard. When you begin the next time quickly revise the letters you have already covered.

### *Keys b and n*

Use **first** finger of left hand on **b**. Use **first** finger of right hand on **n**.

```
fgb jhn fgb jhn  fgb jhn fgb jhn fgb jhn
fbjn fbjn fbjn fbjn fbjn fbjn fbjn fbjn

fen gin ban nib gun ben not bat ran
bone rain join bans bran barn brat knob

the bull and goat are in the barn;
where is our granny; she is in bed;
none of the birds flew in the hail and snow but they did in the
rain
```

### *Keys v and m*

Use **first** finger of left hand on **v**. Use **first** finger of right hand on **m**.

```
fvf jmj fvf jmj fvf jmj fvf jmj fvf jmj
fvbgf jmnhj fvbgf jmnhj fvbgf jmnhj

jam jim gem vim van vet mit vat mat met
mute vain game vein made move vine mine

the mauve jumper was wet and the yellow one dry;
make some jam please; no make orange marmalade;
```

## *Keys c and ,*

Use **first** finger of left hand on **c**. Use **first** finger of right hand on **,** .

```
dcd k,k dcd k,k dcd k,k dcd k,k dcd k,k
decd ki,k decd ki,k decd ki,k decd ki,k
```

One space after a comma:

```
cad, cub, can, cat, act, ace, cab, car,
deck cake race mice tack cane back nice
```

Before typing the following phrases you should set a right-hand margin (see page 12). Set margins of 12 and 88 (10 and 70). Move your carriage, using the carriage release key, towards the right-hand margin. You should hear a bell when the typing point is 5 or 6 spaces from the margin. This warns you while you are typing that you must either begin a new line or divide the next word. If you do not want to divide the word you can use the margin release key to override the margin. This is usually on the left-hand side of the keyboard, marked ↔. As you approach the margin, press it and it will release the margin for that line only.

```
the clown balanced crazily on the back of the horse, then crashed
to the canvas floor;

the rich chocolate cake was much nicer than the coffee one, we
all chose to have a second large slice; then, we were full up;
```

## *Keys x and .*

Use **second** finger of left hand on **x**. Use **second** finger of right hand on **.** .

```
sxs l.l sxs l.l sxs l.l sxs l.l sxs l.l
swxs lo.l swxs lo.l swxs lo.l swxs lo.l
```

The . is used mostly as a full stop. When you type a full stop at the end of a sentence you should leave 2 spaces after it. Try to think of it as part of the word you have just typed.

```
tax.  fix.  six.  mix.  wax.  vex.  lax.
axle axes oxen hoax flex boxes exits extra
```

## Key z

Use **second** finger of left hand on **z**.

```
aza aza aza aza aza aza aza aza aza aza
azxsa azxsa azxsa azxsa azxsa azxsa azxsa
axza axza axza axza axza axza axza axza

zoo zip zoom size ooze jazz seal quiz zero
lazy zebra dizzy zest blaze blazer razor

the lazy zebra lived in a zoo; his coat was always fuzzy and he
liked the sound of jazz.
```

## *Capital letters*

Find the shift key on either side of the keyboard at the bottom. Using the little finger, practise pressing it down. On a manual machine this is quite hard at first.

To get a capital or upper-case letter with a key that you type with the **left** hand, press the **right-hand** shift key.

The sequence is:

1. identify letter
2. press and hold shift key
3. strike required key
4. release shift key

To get a capital or upper-case letter with a key that you type with the **right** hand, press the **left-hand** shift key.

Now, type several times:

```
Aa Bb Cc Dd Ee Ff Gg Hh Ii Jj Kk Ll Mm Nn Oo Pp Qq Rr Ss Tt Uu Vv
Ww Xx Yy Zz ;: ,, ..
```

Your typewriter may have a slightly different keyboard layout for upper case characters, e.g. a question above the comma.

```
Aberdeen, Bournemouth, Chester, Dundee, Ely, Falmouth, Grantham;
Horsham, Ilchester, Jarrow, Kingston, London, Monmouth, Newport;
Oswestry, Preston, Quito, Ripley, Southampton, Tamworth;
Uttoxeter, Yarmouth, Zimbabwe.
```

Remember to leave two spaces after a full stop:

```
Rough.  About.  Brought.  Xanadu.  Touch.
```

You are now ready to learn the top line of the keyboard. Turn to page 21 and continue from there, using the suggested fingering on the chart. If you are still not sure of the position of all the letters, either go back over this chapter or use the slightly different drills in Chapter 1.

# 3 *Consolidation of Keyboard*

The first section is aimed at consolidating your knowledge of the keyboard. Don't forget there is a keyboard plan which you can look at as a quick reminder of the correct finger to use. Type each line at least twice. Leave your mistakes.

## 1 Exercises

```
a   able   are   and   at   away   page   label
banana   pale   malaria   again   avail   axle

be   but   been   bad   bowl   bank   bobble   bangle
bright   beetle   blubber   brain   busby

can   could   coil   crime   chance   change
conceit   concentrate   crown   conscience

do   day   dye   die   dance   drone   decide
deduction   drab   drawer   drop   drown   fade

ever   every   evident   eye   error   effect
enemy   enable   edges   envy   emu   eerie

fine   fate   feudal   frame   follow   fright
friction   for   forty   fourth   fragrant

go   got   give   gave   gift   good   grand
green   grey   gold   cough   bought   grimace

he   hat   hot   high   hole   hymn   bough
clutch   though   through   happy   humour   home

in   ill   it   is   isle   idle   illicit
immediate   iron   introduce   imagine   invalid

jam   jay   jig   just   judge   jog   judgement
jelly   jaunty   justify   jazz   jeopardy

kick   kindle   khaki   kind   knocked   kraken
```

keeled rebuke keep king kingdom

low lend legal light late loosen lose
legislation llama little languid

me must most mine mind mobile more
manage mention moan moisten muse

Go back over this work and mark your errors by putting a circle round them, thus:

me mast most mine mind mebile more

Now retype all the words with errors for practice!

## *Using the shift key and the shift lock*

Leave two spaces after a full stop:

Sunday. Monday. Tuesday. Wednesday. Thursday. Friday.
Saturday.

January. February. March. April. May. June. July.
August. September. October. November. December.

MARTIN CHUZZLEWIT met OLIVER TWIST outside the OLD CURIOSITY SHOP, which was owned by DOMBEY AND SON who lived in BLEAK HOUSE. They went inside and found that DOMBEY was giving a party for DAVID COPPERFIELD who had fallen on HARD TIMES but lived in GREAT EXPECTATIONS that he would make money from the sale of his novel PICKWICK PAPERS.

## *Back to the alphabet*

no now not net noon nobody never
nowhere need next nearly nasty night

out open over only opal object
office ousted ouch often oblivion

put pen pass pity possible probable
possibility perhaps preamble prize

queue quote quiet quicken equal
question aquatic query quantity quality

rat raid rude ready rest archery
reaction right rental rubric really

so shall should send simple shine

```
sleep   singer   sable   sound   sincerely   sent

to   two   too   true   trouble   trust
truthfully   straight   struggle   satisfaction

up   under   usual   undone   university   upset
suite   punctual   uneasy   unable

very   vine   veinous   venus   valve   valuable
verbose   vacancy   valentine   vantage

we   would   were   will   wish   weight
awful   week   weekly   with   without   woven   wine

exit   exeat   axle   mixture   oxen   hexagon
flexible   exacting   excitement   axiom

yes   yet   you   your   young   yours   yesterday
yellow   bicycle   rhythm   yards   ability

zoo   zebra   azalea   ozone   azure   zigzag
zinc   puzzle   crazy   enzyme   zodiac
```

Mark any errors and re-type the words in which they occurred.

### *Common phrases and punctuation*

Remember to leave one space after all punctuation except at the end of a sentence, where you leave two. Type one line of each of the following phrases.

```
We are, as we are, as we were, we are able; have we, we have had,

and we are, we refer to; with reference to, with reference to

your letter.  Yours sincerely, Yours truly, Yours faithfully,

Dear Sir.  Our attention, if there is, your attention: we have

your reply.

Thank you for your letter, from time to time, according to, it is

now, I am very sorry; I shall be glad: as a result, this year, in

the meantime.  Careful consideration, it appears that, at the

same time, for the first time; we look forward.
```

### *Words using e and i, combined with the use of tab stops*

Read the explanation of the tabulator key given on page 85. Clear the margins and tabs.

Set a left-hand margin at 23 and tabs at 33, 45, 57, 67 in elite. Set a left-hand margin at 13 and tabs at 23, 35, 47, 57 in pica.

Go back to the left margin. Use the tab key to check that the stops have been set correctly: each time you press the key the carriage should jump across to the next setting.

Return to the left margin. Type **receive**, press tab key, type **believe**, press tab key, type **eiderdown**, and so on across the first line of the table.

| | | | | |
|---|---|---|---|---|
| receive | believe | eiderdown | vein | fiery |
| serial | friend | prairies | jellied | efficiency |
| duties | supplies | berries | relief | conscience |
| studied | weight | quietly | heinous | reiterate |
| piety | lieu | receipt | feint | weight |

## 2 Paragraphs and line spacing and using the right-hand margin

Up to this point you have been able to follow the line ends given or you have used the margin release key to enable you to complete a word that ran into the right margin.

You should now read pages 48–9 which gives you guidelines for dividing words at the end of a line. You can thus obtain a more even effect on the right-hand side of the page.

Now copy the following paragraphs and make your own right margin. You know that a bell rings within 5 or 6 characters of the margin so that helps you to judge whether a word can be begun or not. An even right margin on the first 2 or 3 lines of any piece of work gives a good visual guide for the rest of the page.

### *Blocked paragraphs*

Insert a sheet of A4 paper. Align the top edge. Turn up one clear inch or 25 mm (7 lines). Set margins of 18 and 88 (15 and

70). Now type the following:

```
This is a blocked paragraph with every line beginning at the
left-hand margin.  You will usually type in single line spacing
and simply return the carriage once at the end of a line.  Then,
when you want to begin a new paragraph, return the carriage twice
to show the break in the text.  Do that now!
```

Check your work for errors and ring any mistakes. See what the right margin looks like. Now re-type the paragraph. Before beginning to type the next paragraph set the line spacing to 2.

```
To type in double line spacing you should first change the

line space lever which is usually on the top left-hand side of

the carriage.  Set on 2 you will get one clear line space between

each line of typing.  Set on 3 you will get two clear line spaces

between each line.  Some machines can also be set at one and a

half.  When using blocked paragraphs, return the carriage twice

before beginning a new paragraph.
```

Check your work, ring any mistakes. Re-type the paragraph.

```
xxxxxxxxxxxxxxxxxxxxx
xxxxxxxxxxxxxxxxxxxxx
xxxxxxxxxxx.

xxxxxxxxxxxxxxxxxxxx
xxxxxxxxxxxxxxxxxxxx
xxxxxxxxxxxx.
```

*Example 3.1. Blocked paragraph, single line spacing. Double line space between paragraphs.*

```
xxxxxxxxxxxxxxxxxxxxx

xxxxxxxxxxxxxxxxxxxxx

xxxxxxxxxxx.



xxxxxxxxxxxxxxxxxxxxx

xxxxxxxxxx.
```

*Example 3.2. Blocked paragraph, double line spacing. Four lines between paragraphs.*

## *Indented paragraphs*

Use the same margins, but set a tab stop 5 spaces in from the left-hand margin. Return the carriage. Single line spacing. Tab to first stop. Type:

```
     An indented paragraph begins 5 spaces in from the left-hand
margin.  The second and subsequent lines begin at the left margin
itself.  When you are typing in single line spacing and want to
begin a new paragraph you simply return the carriage twice and
use the tab key to get the starting point.  Do that now!

     When you have checked your work through and put a ring round
any errors you will be ready to type these two paragaphs again.
```

Before beginning the next paragraphs set the line space lever at 2. Type:

```
     When you type an indented paragraph in double line spacing

it is unnecessary to put an extra space between the paragraphs.

The indented first line makes it quite clear where the new

paragraph begins.
```

Look at the Examples 3.3 and 3.4.

```
     xxxxxxxxxxxxxxxx
xxxxxxxxxxxxxxxxxxxxx
xxxxxxxxxxxxxxxxxxxxx
xxxxxxxxxx.

     xxxxxxxxxxxxxxxx
xxxxxxxxxxxx.
```

*Example 3.3. Indented paragraph, single line spacing. Double line space between paragraphs.*

```
     xxxxxxxxxxxxxxx

xxxxxxxxxxxxxxxxxxxxx

xxxxxxxxxxx.

     xxxxxxxxxxxxxxxxxx

xxxxxxxxxxx.
```

*Example 3.4. Indented paragraph, double line spacing. Double line space between paragraphs.*

## *Words with double letters*

Refer to page 85 for clearing and setting tab stops. Set left margin at 32 and tabs at 45 and 59 in elite type and left margin at 23 with tabs at 36 and 50 in pica.

```
little      dear        carrot
waffle      heartless   lettuce
scatter     hillock     fallacy
accident    omission    paddle
```

Check your errors and re-type.

Now clear the tabs and margin settings. Set left margin at 23 and tabs at 39, 52 and 66 in elite and left margin at 14 with tabs at 30, 43 and 57 in pica.

| | | | |
|---|---|---|---|
| sadness | employee | jagged | yellow |
| warranted | rabbit | narrow | immersion |
| accommodate | wood | affection | illness |
| illegible | vacuum | kitten | happy |

## 3 Paragraph practice

Type each paragraph twice. Once as a blocked paragraph and once as an indented one. Use margins of 18 and 88 (15 and 65). *Type evenly.*

Coffee and tea are popular beverages. Most people have a preference for one and drink several cups of it a day.

Many people have a sweet tooth and like to eat chocolate and biscuits but it seems that sugar is not necessary in our diet.

For health reasons people in Britain are encouraged to eat poly-unsaturated fats - ones made from vegetable oils rather than animal fats.

Bread and potatoes used to be thought 'fattening' but now they are favoured for their high fibre content.

One of the nicest things about sailing out of a harbour on a bright morning with a light breeze is the moment when the engine can be turned off.

Being at sea in a fog is far more unnerving than sailing in rough weather. All the crew have to help as look outs and this involves listening as well.

Manufacturing industry has advanced one stage from automation of assembly lines to using robots for managing and supervising them.

Offices are a little way behind; however, many organizations are beginning to introduce automation to some of their functions.

Once you have a word processor and the right technology it is possible to send messages to someone with compatible equipment.

The introduction of speciality dishes from different nations has meant that various types of restaurant have gone in and out of fashion in recent years.

```
Examples of these fashions in food are Chinese meals, Indian
tandoori dishes, and more recently pizza and pasta from Italy.

People are prepared to travel further and further for their
annual holidays.  The Seychelles seem just as accessible as the
south coast of England does.

It is always worth considering which currencies have a good rate
of exchange against sterling before deciding where you want to
go.

Holidays can be taken almost anywhere in the world quite easily
and package tours are also available to such unlikely places as
the Khyber Pass.

It is well worth persevering to learn the keyboard well because
being able to type accurately is a very useful asset.
```

## 4 Headings

A heading is used to focus attention on what follows in an article, a book, or a table. Typing style can vary:

1. Spaced capitals (3 spaces between words):

   D I F F E R E N T   H E A D I N G S

2. Closed capitals:

   DIFFERENT HEADINGS

3. Initial capitals and underscore:

   <u>Different Headings</u>

Side or shoulder headings are usually typed as in 2 or 3 above.

Paragraph headings can be typed in 2 ways:

<u>Dinard</u>  This resort is on the coast

Here the heading is on the same line as the beginning of the paragraph.

<u>Dinard</u> is a resort

In this example the heading forms the beginning of the sentence.

In the Example 3.5 all of these headings are used. Type it using margins of 24 and 76 (20 and 60).

```
B R I T T A N Y
                                         Main headings
NORTH-WEST FRANCE

The Coast                                Shoulder heading

This part of France has a rocky coastline
with many bays and inlets.  There are
miles of sandy beaches and coastal paths
to be walked and they give constantly
changing views as one goes from bay to bay.

Dinard is a resort developed in Edwardian   Paragraph heading
times on one of the loveliest bays of
what is known as the Emerald Coast.
```

*Example 3.5*

By now you should be typing quite accurately, but when you make mistakes you will want to be able to correct them. This has not been introduced earlier because correcting errors when you are making a great many is very time consuming. You should now read pages 47–8 and then re-type the passage above, making any corrections as you go along.

## 5 Inferior and superior characters

You may need to type symbols where the character is raised above the typing line (superior), or where it is lowered (inferior). For superior, turn the platen knob *one* notch anticlockwise and for inferior, *one* notch clockwise. Thus:

$H^2O$ $H_2SO_4$ $32^oF$ $100^oC$ $x^2$

Remember to turn the platen back again when you have finished.

## 6 Time

Be consistent in the way you present time. The 24-hour clock has no punctuation while in the 12-hour clock minutes and hours are separated by a full stop, but there is no punctuation in am and pm. Now type the following:

```
1215 hrs   2129 hrs   12.15 am   9.29 pm   12 midnight

The train arrived at 2105 hrs instead of 2055 hrs.  I am going
to meet  Jane at 11.15 am tomorrow at Paddington and she will
leave on Saturday by the 9.30 am train which gets her home
at 3.25 pm.
```

## 7 Carriage return drill

Practise returning the carriage as quickly as you can. Type the following exactly as it is shown:

```
Practise
Practise returning
Practise returning the
Practise returning the carriage
Practise returning the carriage quickly.

This
This saves
This saves you
This saves you time.
```

You can do this exercise using any sentence you like, and it is useful practice on an electric/electronic keyboard as well as a manual one.

## 8 Use of words and figures

Read and then type the following sentence:

```
One man detached himself from the other 6 and gave the 1st
indication of the views of the group.
```

One should always be typed as a word and any figure beginning a sentence should be typed as a word. Figures can be used anywhere else in a sentence. First, second, third etc. can be typed either as shown in the above sentence or as words.

## 9 Typing abbreviations

In *open* punctuation full stops are omitted. Type the following for practice:

J Smith MA BSc JP

We go to London frequently, viz Monday, Tuesday and Thursday each week.

PS  Please send the cheque you owe me.

The coat comes in several colours, eg red, green, black.

BBC and ITV transmit news programmes at 9.0 pm and 10.0 pm respectively.

An inch is equal to 25 mm and 1½" to 38 mm.

My car has a 1287 cc engine, yours has a 2.61 engine.

Be careful that a sentence looking like the one below in draft form is typed up as in 1, not 2.

On 27/9/85 we shd all be at t circus.

1. On 27 September 1985 we should all be at the circus. ✓

2. On 27/9/85 we shd all be at the circus. ✗

## 10 Consolidation

Use margins of 1½ in or 38 mm. Type each paragraph twice. Keep as straight a right-hand margin as you can, and make corrections in your work.

Spring is a time when the buds on all the trees begin to swell. The weeping willow is one of the first to show that winter is coming to an end as the bright green leaves show through on the branches.

English gardens in summer are often a riot of colour because of the number of flowers as well as the varieties grown. June is the month when roses first appear and it is common to see them still blooming as late as October.

During the autumn, or the 'fall', the countryside displays a range of different hues: green, yellow, bronze, red and brown. The leaves on the trees change colour before dropping on to the ground to form a carpet.

Although in winter there is little colour in the garden or the country, the plants are preparing for spring. However, the outlines of the trees make interesting shapes against the grey skies, and evergreens look pretty with snow on their branches, turning the dreariest garden into a fairyland.

Change your margins to 1 in or 25 mm. Type the following in double line spacing. Check with pages 37–8 before beginning.

Typewriters have changed a great deal since they first became available commercially in the latter part of the last century. The aspect that has not changed is the layout of the keyboard, although in fact it would be possible to have one that was more economical of hand movement.

When electric typewriters first came on to the market they were only very slightly different from a manual machine. The main change was the introduction of a key for the carriage return function. The keys themselves were still arranged in a type basket.

Single element machines are now more common. Instead of a type basket, the characters are located either on a golf ball head or a daisy wheel. It is simple to change to a different type face or print size. Recent developments have been in the area of electronic machines which are reputed to be more reliable as they have few moving parts; many of these machines have small memories and LCD display panels which makes it possible to view and correct script before it is printed on to the page.

## 11 Speed development

You may like to know how fast you can type. Speed is worked out on 'average' or 'standard' word length. This consists of 5 strokes or spaces. A typing line of 40 characters gives 8 standard words. There are a number of books on the market which are aimed at speed development and have practice passages marked out in strokes per line. If you want or need this type of practice you could either borrow such a book from the local library or buy your own copy. However, there is also some material marked out in this way on pages 129–32.

A very good way of improving speed is to use material with which you are already familiar. You could repeat some of the drills and practice paragraphs given in these first chapters.

Begin by timing yourself for 1 minute, then add a minute at a time until you have reached 5 minutes. If the passage you are using is not long enough, simply start it again.

Type the sentence below as many times as you can in 2 minutes. Work out the number of strokes you have typed by using the figures given in the right-hand margin. Divide by 5 for standard words, then divide again for the number of minutes you have been typing (this time by 2).

Example 1

```
The quick brown fox jumped over the lazy dog.            44
```

Example 2

```
Now is the time for all good men to come to the aid of the party. 66
```

Mark the errors you have made by circling them. More than 5% of error is not really acceptable in speed tests. That means that for every 20 words, you should not make more than one mistake!

# 4 *The Perfect Page*

## 1 Making corrections

There are many materials on the market for making corrections if the machine you have does not have a self-correcting facility.

The easiest material to use is correcting paper. Initially you will only need to buy it in white but it is also possible to buy coloured correcting paper for use on carbon copies.

Ideally you will also buy some liquid correcting fluid and this is available in a range of colours as well as white.

There are occasions when correcting paper gives better results than the liquid and vice versa.

### *Correcting with paper*

When you see that you have made an error take the typing point back to the error. Insert the paper between the ribbon and the paper and type the incorrect letter again. When you remove the paper the letter should have disappeared. Backspace one and type in the correct letter.

### *Correcting with liquid*

It is better to use liquid when you want to take out a word and not type anything in its place. The same applies to removing punctuation. Simply paint over the error and let the paint dry. You do need to ensure that you don't move the carriage too quickly and so get paint all over the bail bar and guide card etc. Be certain that the liquid is kept fairly thin – a thinner can be bought to dilute the correction fluid – or else your work will look a little like an oil painting!

Carbon copy correction is explained on page 66.

### *Making corrections and replacing the paper in the machine*

Use liquid to erase the error. Sometimes it is easier to delete a whole word rather than just an odd letter. Put the sheet of paper back into the machine and carefully align the line of typing with the alignment scale.

Put the typewriter on to stencil, i.e. disengage the ribbon. If your typewriter uses a ribbon cassette, take it out. Now type in the correction – you will only get an impression – and check that it is in the right place. Either make another alignment adjustment or re-engage the ribbon (or cassette) and type in the missing letter.

If you find that your work is not quite correct vertically (the letters do not fall under those above), you could try using the half-space key, if your machine has one. Backspace to the letter before the one to be corrected, press the half-space key and hold it down while you insert the letter to be replaced.

## 2 Division of words

Simple rules for the division of words at the end of a line are as follows:

1. Follow the sound. Resignation is pronounced **resig-nation** not resign-ation and should be divided accordingly.
2. Divide after a prefix or before a suffix: **Con-centrate, second-ment**.
3. Divide double consonants: **tran-quil, trem-bled** (here consider point 1 above as well), **chil-dren** but not child-ren.

   Divide between the repeated consonant of words which have double consonants: **run-ning, sit-ting** *but* **tell-ing**.

Do not divide the following categories of words:

1. Words of one syllable, i.e. where there is only one stressed vowel sound: **cause, groom, black**.
2. Words that already have a hyphen in them: **self-confident, co-operative**.

3. Sets of numbers and initials: **3″×2″×5″**, **BBC**, **£500,000**.
4. Places and persons. Also, do not split a person's name from his/her title: **Edinburgh**, **Yugoslavia**, **Mr John Smith**.
5. From the point of view of typing style it is preferable not to divide:
   a) so that you split the last word of a paragraph
   b) so that you split the last word on a page
   c) so that 3 lines in a row have word divisions
   d) so that you are left with 2 letters either at the end of one line or the beginning of the next

## 3 Combination characters

Some keyboards do not provide all the characters, although most modern electronic machines have the majority. Some characters can be typed by combining 2 keys. Type the first character, backspace, and then type the second character over the first, making alignment adjustments as necessary.

| | |
|---|---|
| ⋇ | Asterisk: **x** and – |
| ÷ | Division sign: **:** and – |
| = | Equals sign: – turn platen knob one notch then type second – |
| – | Plus sign: – and draw in vertical |
| $ | Dollar sign: **S** and / |
| ¢ | Cent sign: **c** and / |
| ! | Exclamation sign: ' and . |
| ‡ | Dagger: **I** and – |
| /‾ _/ | Square backets: *Opening bracket:* solidus, backspace and underscore. Turn platen knob anticlockwise *two* notches, underscore. *Closing backet:* solidus, backspace *twice*, underscore, turn platen knob anticlockwise *two* notches, underscore. |

If you have to adjust the platen knob, always remember to return to the original line of typing afterwards.

## 4 Use of upper case on top line of the keyboard

* (Asterisk) In footnotes, both as a text indicator:

```
... delete*
```

and at the bottom of the page:

```
* Delete as applicable
```

Footnotes should be indented 1 or 2 spaces and typed in blocked style, so that if there are several of them, the asterisks stand proud of the notes (see page 126).

/ (Solidus) Wherever it is used there should be no space on either side of it. If you do not have the fraction you need on the keyboard you can compile it with the solidus:

```
1/2          7/8      his/hers    Dear Sir/Madam
```

@ Principally used for invoicing. Stands for 'at':

```
12 books @ £20
```

**£** (Libra) Used to show amounts of money (see page 111).

**&** (Ampersand) In the inside name and address on a letter:

```
Mr & Mrs J Smith  Brown & Black Brothers
          32 & 33 Wells Street
```

It should not be used in running text as a substitute for 'and'.

" (Speech marks) In text where direct quotations are used.

```
"Please contact us next week," he said.
```

' (Apostrophe) To show the omission of a letter and in possessives:

```
Don't (do not)  It's (it is)
London's biggest theatre
Doctors' surgeries
```

# 5 *Letters*

## 1 Laying out business letters

A business letter contains a number of different parts, and can be produced in several styles. The simplest layout is the *fully-blocked style* where all the various parts of the letter begin at the left-hand margin. It is also easiest to use open punctuation everywhere except in the body of the letter. This means that all non-essential punctuation is omitted.

The numbers of the following elements of a business letter correspond to those in the margin of Figure 5.1.

**1 Reference** Placed 2 or 3 lines below printed heading. It is frequently made up of writer's and typist's initials: **JB/GS** (writer/typist) or may refer to a file number: **GS/3784** (writer/customer file).

Sometimes you need to quote your own reference and the reference that appeared on the letter being answered:

**Our ref GS/3784**
**Your ref RT/3890**

All business letters should carry a reference so that they can be traced back to their source if necessary.

**2 Date** This should be put in full and the order is day, month, year: **14 January 1988, 22 April 1991, 1 October 2000.** Do not use 12/1/85, 22/4/91 or 1/10/2001.

**3 Inside name and address** either

**Mr John Buchanan**
**19 Lionel Hill**
**FEATHERSTONE**
**South Yorks PT9 FT6**

or

WALKER & REID PLC
82 High Lane
GRANTHAM
Lincs GR9 2HL

1 Your Ref JB/GS

2 14 January 1988

3 John Buchanan Esq
19 Lionel Hill
FEATHERSTONE
South Yorks PT9 FT6

4 Dear Mr Buchanan

5 I received your letter of 12 January this morning. As I was unable to contact you on the telephone I am writing to confirm that next Tuesday, 22 January, at approximately 2.30 pm will be quite convenient for you to call and take measurements. After that I understand that you will send an estimate in writing.

6 Yours sincerely
7 (name of firm)

8 John Smith
9 OFFICE MANAGER

10 Enc.

Figure 5.1

**John Buchanan Esq**
**19 Lionel Hill**
**FEATHERSTONE**
**South Yorks PT9 FT6**

**4 Salutation** either **Dear Sir** or **Dear Mr Buchanan**.

**5 Body of letter** This example is typed using blocked paragraphs and in single spacing. The punctuation is as in normal English usage.

**6 Complimentary close** Linked with the style of the salutation: either **Yours sincerely** with 'Dear Mr Buchanan' or **Yours faithfully** or **Yours truly** with 'Dear Sir/s'.

**7 Name of firm** If inserted, typed immediately under complimentary close:

**Yours faithfully**
**WALKER & REID plc**

or

**Yours sincerely**
**Walker & Reid plc**

**8 Name** Name of the person writing the letter: either **John Smith** or **GILL SUGDEN (MISS)**.

**9 Designation** If the writer has a particular function in the company this information can be given: either

**John Smith**
**Office Manager**

or

**JOHN SUGDEN**
**OFFICE MANAGER (or Office Manager)**

**10 Enclosures** It is usual to indicate whether anything is enclosed with the letter by typing either **Enc.** or **Encs.**

You should now be able to type a letter. Use A4 paper (see page 5). If you use plain paper, turn up 12 lines to allow for a printed heading.

Set the margins at 1½ ins or 38 mm, i.e. 18 and 82 on an elite machine, 15 and 65 on a pica machine.

If you use headed paper, the margins can be set to line up with the edge of the printing in the heading.

Insert top of sheet, heading away from you, into the machine. Wind paper round and turn up appropriate amount (see page 51).

The bold numbers on the left of Example 5.1 indicate the number of carriage returns between items.

## *Points of layout to check*

Remember the visual appearance of the finished typescript is important.

Your finished letter should look like (a) in Figure 5.2. If it looks like (b) the right-hand margin is too wide. Keep to even margins. If it looks like (c) then *either* your letter could have been typed on a smaller sheet of paper *or* you should leave more space between the parts of the letter. That is, increase the space below the reference, date, and inside name and address to 3 clear lines. (Return carriage 4 times.)

The spacing between items can be adjusted but these spaces should be consistent within one letter.

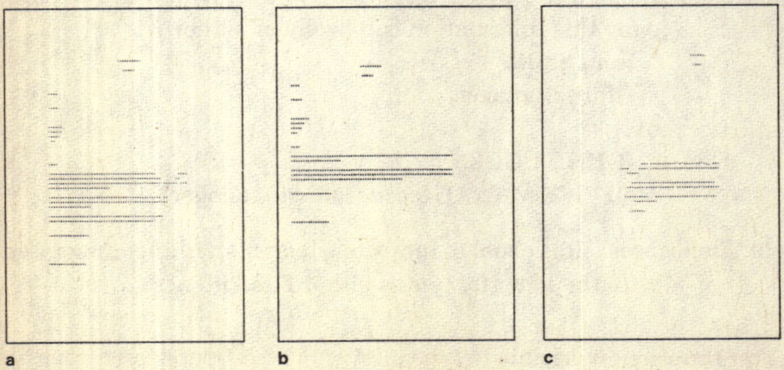


Figure 5.2

Ref JB/GS

3

12 January 1988

3

John Smith Esq
Walker & Reid plc
82 High Lane
GRANTHAM
Lincs GR9 2HL

3

Dear Mr Smith

2

Thank you for your letter which I received this morning. I shall be delighted to visit your offices, in order to measure the windows for thermally-lined curtains, and to advise you on suitable carpets. If it is convenient I shall call next Tuesday, 22 January, as I shall be in your area on that day.

2

You will receive my written estimate by the end of next week, and if you do wish to place an order I shall be able to undertake the work during the second week of February.

2

I look forward to meeting you.

2

Yours sincerely

6

John Buchanan

*Example 5.1*

### *Using unheaded paper*

If you do not have printed paper you can put your own address at the top of the page. There are 2 methods to choose from shown in Figure 5.3. In (a) simply type from the left-hand margin.

To place typing as in (b) so that you get a justified right-hand margin, take the typing point to the right-hand margin setting, then backspace *once* for each character and each space in the line. (Spell it to yourself and backspace at the same time.) Then, type in the line.

The letter in Example 5.2 can be typed on A5 paper (see page 59). Use margins of 9 and 61 on an elite machine and 7 and 43 on a pica machine. All the points relating to A4 letters apply here.

Again, check your letter for appearance against the layout diagrams on page 54.

## 2 Envelopes

The name and address which appear on the envelope should correspond to the name and address on the letter. The typing should be in the bottom half of the envelope to allow space for the Post Office cancellation stamp or franking mark. Pinch a mark at the left-hand edge before you insert the envelope into the machine to give yourself a visual guide.

Aim to have the longest line roughly centred across the width of

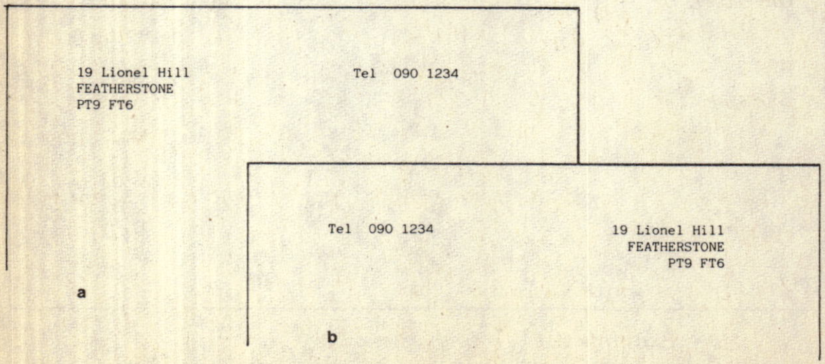


*Figure 5.3*

WALKER & REID PLC
82 High Lane
GRANTHAM
Lincs GR9 2HL

Your Ref JB/GS

14 January 1988

John Buchanan Esq
19 Lionel Hill
FEATHERSTONE
South Yorks PT9 FT6

Dear Mr Buchanan

I received your letter of 12 January this morning. As I was unable to contact you on the telephone I am writing to confirm that next Tuesday, 22 January, at approximately 2.30 pm will be quite convenient for you to call and take measurements. After that I understand that you will send an estimate in writing.

Yours sincerely

John Smith
OFFICE MANAGER

*Example 5.2*

the envelope. As a rough guide you can begin 2 ins from the left edge on a small envelope and 2¼ ins on a larger one. Practise on folded pieces of paper to begin with. Address an envelope as shown in Example 5.3 on page 58.

You will find a list of addresses for copying practice on pages 149–50.

Letters to be sent overseas retain the same style; the country appears in capitals:

Mr John Smith
Walker & Reid plc
82 High Lane
GRANTHAM
Lincs GR9 2HL
ENGLAND

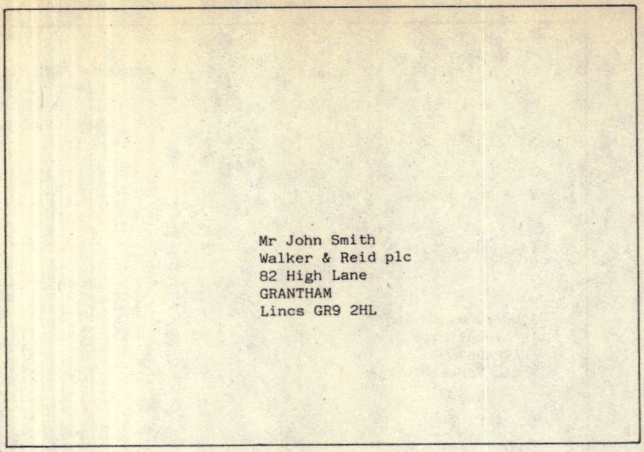


*Example 5.3*

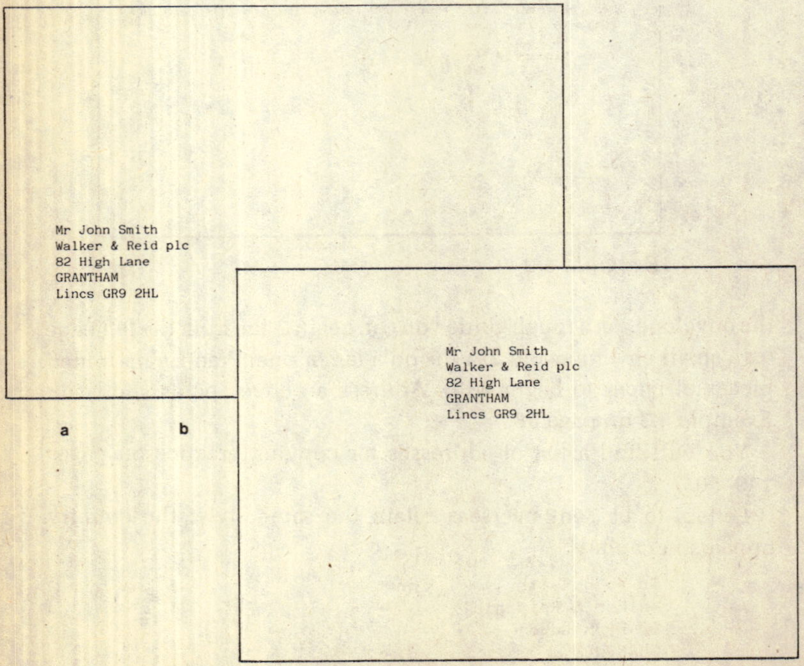


*Figure 5.4*

Some thicker and larger types of envelope may not feed easily through the machine. You may therefore find it easier to type the address on to a label and stick it on the envelope.

Avoid making the mistakes shown in Figure 5.4. (a) has the address too far to the left; in (b) it is too high and will be covered by Post Office franking.

## 3 Paper and envelope sizes

Paper sizes are prefixed by an A and are based on a rectangle which retains similar proportions each time it is halved as shown in Figure 5.5. The sizes that you are likely to use in business are A6 (postcards), A5 (short letters) and A4 (letters).

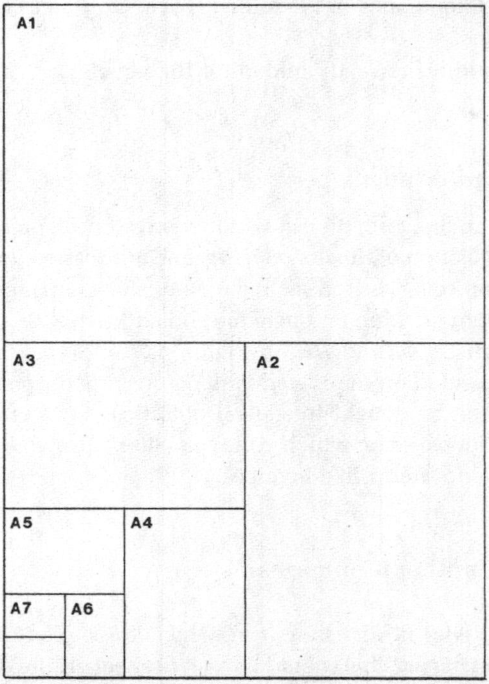


Figure 5.5

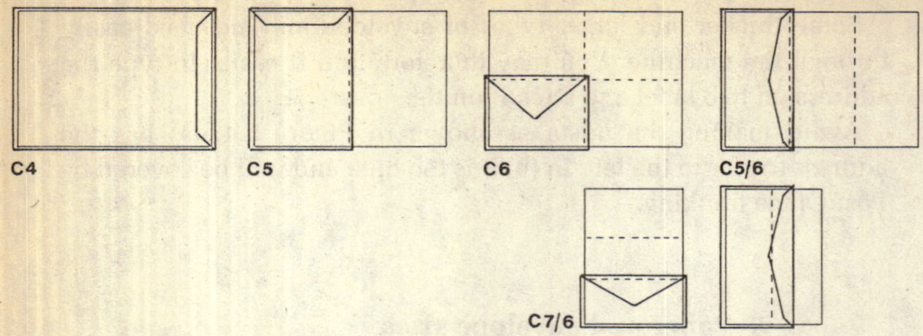


*Figure 5.6*

Envelopes are shown in Figure 5.6. C4 takes a sheet of A4 flat; C5 takes a sheet of A5 flat or A4 folded once; C6 takes a sheet of A5 folded once or A4 folded twice; C5/6 (often a window envelope) takes a sheet of A5 folded once or A4 folded twice; C7/6 takes a sheet of A5 folded twice.

Letters should be correctly folded for the envelope that is being used.

### *Window envelopes*

If you are going to use window envelopes you may have to adjust the position of the inside name and address on your letter. Put the envelope over the top section of your sheet of paper in order to judge the right position for the name and address. It should all be visible through the window as in Figure 5.7(b). Some firms have guide marks printed on their headed paper for this purpose.

Envelopes can be bought in several qualities. Try to match the envelopes to the paper on which you type letters. Brown envelopes should be used for items like invoices.

## 4 Continuation pages

If a letter is very long it may have to be continued on a second sheet of paper. This should be a *plain* sheet of similar quality to the first or headed sheet. Set the page out as in Figure 5.8.

a

b

*Figure 5.7*

Remember the overall appearance of the work. Don't have one line of a paragraph on either the bottom of the first page or the top of the second.

12 January 1988

John Smith Esq

xxxxxxxxxxxxxxxxxxxxxxxxxxxxxxxxxxxxxxxxxxxxxxxxxxxxxxxxxxxx
xxxxxxxxxxxxxxxxxxxxxxxxxxxxxxxxxxxxxxxxxxxxxxxxxxxxxxxxxxxx
xxxxxxxxxxxxxxxxxx

Yours sincerely

John Buchanan
OFFICE MANAGER

*Figure 5.8*

## 5 Letters with subject headings

Many business letters have a subject heading. This enables the recipient to see quickly to which case or file the letter refers. The heading is placed after the salutation and before the main body of the letter.

Example 5.4 is a letter with a subject heading. It can be typed on a sheet of A5 paper.

12 Lockesley Square

Idmiston Road

SURBITON

GS

20 January 1988

Mr James McTavish
Castles - Estate Agents
101 Fulham Road
LONDON SW6 4QR

Dear Mr McTavish

2

12 KINGS ROAD LONDON SW3 1LN

2

I am writing to confirm that I wish to go ahead with the purchase of the above property. I am, therefore, enclosing a cheque for £500 as an initial deposit. I shall be forwarding the name and address of my solicitor in a few days' time.

Yours faithfully

Gill Sugden (Miss)

Enc

Ref

*Example 5.4*

## 6 For the attention of

Sometimes correspondence is addressed to a company, but because the writer actually knows the contact it is marked for that person's attention (Example 5.5). The letter in Example 5.1 could have been addressed in this way.

## 7 Private and confidential

You may want a letter to go directly to the person to whom it is addressed in a company, and not be opened by anyone else. In that case insert a PRIVATE AND CONFIDENTIAL line as in Figure 5.9.

```
      Ref
2
      Date
2
      PRIVATE AND CONFIDENTIAL
2
      Castles - Estate Agents
      101 Fulham Road
      LONDON SW6 4QR
2
      FOR THE ATTENTION OF MR JAMES McTAVISH
2
```

*Figure 5.9*

## 8 Taking a carbon copy

It is usual to keep a file copy of all business letters. You can do this by using carbon paper. Generally the copy is taken on coloured bank paper (also called 'flimsy' because of its lightness) and kept in the relevant customer's file.

Carbon paper can be bought in varying qualities and colours. The heavier the paper the more copies can be taken, and the longer the paper will last.

Make up a carbon pack on the desk beside the typewriter as shown in Figure 5.10. Put your thumbs under the pack, 1st to 3rd fingers

12 Lockesley Square

Idmiston Road

SURBITON

GS

20 January 1988

3

Castles - Estate Agents
101 Fulham Road
LONDON SW6 4QR

3

FOR THE ATTENTION OF MR JAMES McTAVISH

Dear Sirs

12 KINGS ROAD LONDON SW3 1LN

I am writing to confirm that I wish to go ahead with the purchase of the above property. I am, therefore, enclosing a cheque for £500 as an initial deposit. I shall be forwarding the name and address of my solicitor in a few days' time.

Yours faithfully

Gill Sugden (Miss)

Enc

*Example 5.5*

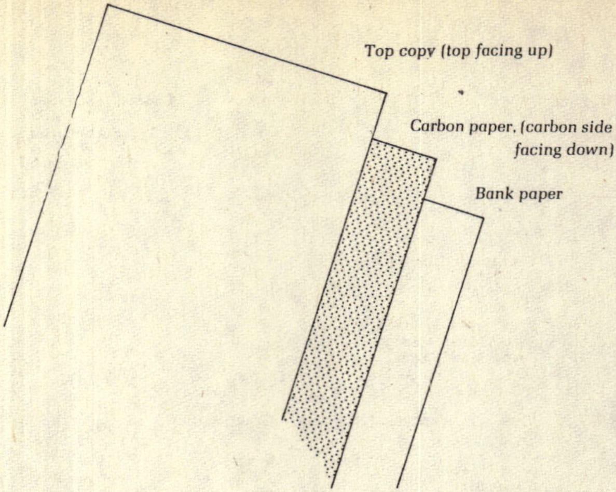


Figure 5.10

on top, and insert pack between rollers. Once the papers have been wound through use the paper release key to adjust the top edges of the papers so that they are even.

You can take extra copies (usually up to about 6) by using alternate sheets of carbon and bank paper. If your machine has a pressure control, adjust this to high. It is likely to be a + – sign, or a set of numbers. (Consult the typing manual.)

Now type the letter in the normal way. You may not consider it worth correcting a single character which is wrong. However, to make a correction either insert a piece of correcting paper between carbon and copy, or use a typing rubber on the copy. (If you do this you must correct each copy individually beginning with the top copy. Before beginning to erase put a scrap of rough paper between each carbon and its copy. Remember to take them out as you go!)

If you send copies of a letter to a number of people, you should list their names at the foot of the letter in the same way as on memos (see page 79). You can also send blind carbon copies of letters (again see page 80).

## 9 Letters with displayed material

The body of a letter may contain information which would be clearer if displayed, either in columns or in numbered paragraphs.

In Example 5.6 the prices of boats have been set out in columns:

19 June 1988

J W Dransfield Esq
82 Goldhawk Lane
LONDON SW6 5DA

Dear Mr Dransfield

Thank you for your telephone call of yesterday inquiring about second-hand boats at present in our yards, and between 35' and 40' in length. We have several boats for sale at the present time, two of them being on our moorings in the Channel Islands.

1 AT SOUTHAMPTON

| | | | | | |
|---|---|---|---|---|---|
| 2 | MODEL | LOA | BEAM | PRICE | YEAR |
| 3 | Moody | 36' | 9'3" | £33500 | 1982 |
| | Mirage | 37' | 10'6" | £50000 | 1984 |
| | She | 35' | 8'9" | £26000 | 1980 |
| | Rival 34 | 34'2" | 8'3" | £29000 | 1980 |

4 AT CHANNEL ISLAND MOORINGS

| | | | | | |
|---|---|---|---|---|---|
| 5 | Contessa | 40' | 9'8" | £37000 | 1981 |
| | Jeanneau | 38'3" | 12'7" | £42950 | 1984 |

Prices are inclusive of any VAT payable.

We are pleased to be able to offer a 5% discount as the proposed purchase is for a club. Should you wish to have a sea trial on any of the above boats, or should you have any queries, please do not hesitate to telephone me. The relevant layout and inventory details are enclosed.

We look forward to hearing from you.

Yours sincerely
SEAHORSE BOATYARDS

Charles Chichester

Enc

*Example 5.6*

In letters with a number of columns and if each column is fairly wide, you may have to narrow the margins accordingly, perhaps to 12 and 94 (10 and 75). In Example 5.6, however, which has narrow columns, wider margins such as 18 and 88 (15 and 70) can be used.

Clear the tab stops on the typewriter (see page 85 or your manual). Type the letter down to the beginning of the displayed section. Return the carriage twice and type the heading marked 1. Return the carriage.

Decide which is the longest line in each column, including any headings. (Remember feet and inch symbols take up a space.) In this case it is: **Jeanneau** (8 spaces), **38′3″** (5), **12′7″** (5), **£42950** (6), **1984** (4).

Now make sure you know how to set tab stops (see page 85 or your typewriter manual). Then, starting from the left-hand margin, tap out on the space bar one space for each letter of the longest line of column 1 (Jeanneau); allow 5 spaces between columns. *Set a tab.* Tap out column 2 and again leave 5 spaces. *Set a tab.* Repeat this for columns 4 and 5.

Return the carriage and type in the 5 headings marked **2**. Type: **MODEL** (press tab key), **LOA** (press tab key), **BEAM** etc.

Leave a clear line before typing the details at **3**.

Type *across* the page, not *down* the columns. Be careful of alignment in column 3.

Leave a clear line before typing heading **4** and, again, a clear line before the details at **5**.

As with previous letters remember the final appearance. Don't crowd headings and details; make sure they stand out. You can always use a continuation page.

## 10 Letters with displayed paragraphs

Sometimes information in a letter is clearer if it is set out in numbered paragraphs, or under a shoulder heading, rather than as continuous prose. The letter below shows numbered paragraphs, where it is easier for the recipient to ensure that when answering the letter all the points raised are clarified.

The simplest way of typing a letter of this kind is to number the paragraph and then tap in 2 or 3 spaces from the number before typing each item. (On some electronic machines you can set a temporary margin for this and use the margin release to insert the numbers.)

The letter in Example 5.7(a) can be typed on A5 paper with margins of 9 and 61 (7 and 43).

Another acceptable layout for the displayed part of the letter is given below but it is not so clear as the numbers do not stand out

1 How many berths do you need in the caravan?

2 Do you intend to tow the caravan or keep it permanently at the same site?

3 What range of cooking facilities do you hope to find in the caravan?

29 May 1988

Mrs M James
53 Rayleigh Road
DARLINGTON
Co Durham DA6 DU1

Dear Mrs James

Thank you for your letter inquiring about our range of caravans. Before sending you a selection of our brochures it would be helpful if you would answer the following queries.

1. How many berths do you need in the caravan?

2. Do you intend to tow the caravan or keep it permanently at the same site?

3. What range of cooking facilities do you hope to find in the caravan?

As soon as we receive your letter we shall dispatch details of our range which most suit your needs.

Yours sincerely
COMANCHE CARAVANS

Gill Sugden

*Example 5.7(a)*

29 May 1988

Mrs M James
53 Rayleigh Road
DARLINGTON
Co Durham DA6 DU1

Dear Mrs James

Thank you for your letter inquiring about our range of caravans. Before sending you a selection of our brochures it would be helpful if you would answer the following queries.

1 How many berths do you need in the caravan?

2 Do you intend to tow the caravan or keep it permanently at the same site?

3 What range of cooking facilities do you hope to find in the caravan?

As soon as we receive your letter we shall dispatch details of our range which most suit your needs.

Yours sincerely
COMANCHE CARAVANS

Gill Sugden

*Example 5.7 (b)*

Some people like to indent the numbers ½ in from the left-hand margin, as shown in Example 5.7(b). In all three examples you will see that the numbered paragraphs are brought in from the right-hand margin. This is a matter of preference.

In Example 5.8 details in continuous prose have to be separated from each other. The most convenient way to do this is to use shoulder headings (see pages 41–2). Suitable margins for this letter would be 18 and 88 (15 and 70). The letter could also be set out with paragraph headings (see pages 41–2).

24 March 1988

Ms Margo Yackimchick BSc
156 Long Wood Road
Battersea
LONDON SW17 3QR

Dear Ms Yackimchick

Thank you for your recent inquiry about secretarial courses at our College. Three of those which we run would, I think, be suitable for you, and I give the details below.

Six Month Intensive

This course aims to get the student to an employable standard in the skills of shorthand, typewriting and word processing. This aspect of the work takes 90% of the course time. The remainder of the teaching week includes work on secretarial duties and commercial English. All students spend one week of their course in the College's model office.

One Year Full-Time Secretarial Course

This course leads to students taking the Private Secretary's Certificate of the London Chamber of Commerce. As well as studying the skills students also study background to business. During the course all students have a two week period of work experience arranged for them.

One Year Full-Time Personal Assistants Course for Graduates

On this course about 50% of the time is spent studying the secretarial skills, and students also receive a thorough grounding in information technology with particular stress on word processing. The remainder of the course includes such subjects as background economics and organizational studies, and a choice between commercial law and accounting.

I enclose an application form for you to complete should you wish to study with us in the next academic year.

Yours sincerely

Winifred Hunt
College Secretary

Enc

*Example 5.8*

## 11 Circular letters

Sometimes the same letter has to be sent to a number of people. For example, during an advertising campaign, or as a reminder letter about payment of a bill where the only item that varies is the amount due. In the first example it is likely that you would either run a mail merge program on a word processor, or have it done through an agency. The letter would be stored on one file, the address list on a second file, and the computer instructed to merge the two files. In this way the letter can quite easily be personalized, and variables can be inserted at appropriate places. This means that the letter can begin Dear Mr instead of Dear Sir, and the amount overdue, as in the second example, can be entered as a different amount for each customer.

However, if you want to type a master letter which can then be photocopied as needed, the usual layout is as Figure 5.11, with the following elements.

**1** Date either **Date as Postmark** or Month Year, e.g. **June 1988**.

**2** Leave space for name and address (8–10 lines).

**3** Salutation can be **Dear Sir/Madam**; **Dear Sir**; **Dear Madam**; or, if personalized, **Dear Mr** followed by space for name to be inserted.

**4** Signature. Top copy to be signed: although occasionally each copy will be signed individually, for instance if the letter is to important clients.

Type the circular letter (Example 5.9, page 74) on A4 paper. Use margins of 1½ ins. Once you have typed the letter, take two copies and insert the following names and addresses in the space provided.

**William Deacon Esq**
**27 Acorn Avenue**
**KINGSTON UPON THAMES**

**John Brightwell Esq**
**326 Western Avenue**
**EALING W5**

PRINTED HEADING

1 Date

2

3 Salutation

xxxxxxxxxxxxxxxxxxxxxxxxxxxxxxxxxxxxxxxxxxxxxxxxxxxxxxxxxxxxxxxxxxxx
xxxxxxxxxxxxxxxxxxxxxxxxxx.

xxxxxxxxxxxxxxxxxxxxxxxxxxxxxxxxxxxxxxxxxxxxxxxxxxxxxxxxxxxxxxxxxxxx
xxxxxxxxxxxxxxxxxxxxxxxxxxxxxxxx.

Complimentary Close
Company Name

4

Name
Designation

Figure 5.11

FUN SKIING

ST ANN'S SQUARE

MANCHESTER

Date as Postmark

Dear Sir

We are delighted to send you our new brochure for 'FUN SKIING' in Winter 1988/89. As you will see we have been able to keep our prices at the same levels as last year.

Our holidays now have a reputation for their excellent 'all-in' value, and because of this we anticipate heavy bookings. May I take this opportunity of advising you that it would be best to book early and so avoid unnecessary disappointment.

We look forward to planning your next skiing holiday in the near future.

Yours faithfully

Julian Dransfield
MANAGER - SKIING HOLIDAYS

*Example 5.9*

**Adrian Blythe Esq**
**St Govan's**
**Lancaster Avenue**
**CHELMSFORD Essex**

## 12 Tear-off forms

Circular letters often have a tear-off form at the bottom of the page to be completed and returned to the sender.

Type this form in double line spacing so that there is ample space for the replies. Leave sufficient space for the address and postcode.

The form may be set out as in Figure 5.12 on page 76.

1. Use spaced hyphens from edge to edge of paper.
2. Type name, leave 2 spaces before typing line of dots ending at right-hand margin.
3. Leave 2 clear spaces after dots and prior to next word.

Type Example 5.10 (page 77), using margins of 18 and 88 (15 and 70). If you are uncertain about how much space the tear-off form will take, it is easy to work it out. Count up the number of lines to be used in the form and add on 4–6 more for the bottom margin. Convert this to the number of inches it will use. (Remember 6 lines of typing to 1 in or 25 mm.) Then simply measure up from the bottom of the page and put a light pencil mark at the edge of the paper. That will be the point where the tear-off line should be placed.

## 13 Memorandums

Memorandums or memos can be described as internal letters. They are used to give or request information or to confirm conversations. A memo is not sent by external mail but put in an internal envelope and delivered to another part of the building by hand. In larger organizations it may be sent to different buildings, or different parts of the country by way of an internal mailing service.

Usually a memo is typed on a pre-printed form but it is easy to

PRINTED HEADING

Date

Salutation

xxxxxxxxxxxxxxxxxxxxxxxxxxxxxxxxxxxxxxxxxxxxxxxxxxxxxxxxxxxxxxxxxxxx
xxxxxxxxxxxxxxxxxxxxxxxxxxxxxxxxxxxxxxxxxxxxxxxxxxxxxxxxxxxxxxxxxxxx
xxxxxxxxxxxxxxxxxxxxxxxxxxxxxxxx.

Complimentary Close

- - - - - - - - - - - - - - - - - - - - - - - - - - - - - - - - - - - -

Name ..........................................................

Address .......................................................

Date ..................... Signature ..........................

Figure 5.12

C I T Y   G A R D E N   S O C I E T Y

Please reply to

85 Kings Road
LONDON SE5 KR7

January 1988

Dear Member

Once again it is time for me to write enclosing details of our Annual General Meeting which is to be held on 29 March 1988, at the Central Hall, Westminster. As you will see the business part of the meeting will be held in the morning. After a buffet lunch we have two speakers well-known for their innovative ideas on planning and landscaping gardens in cities.

May I ask you to complete the tear-off slip below and return it to me at the above address not later than 30 January. This letter also gives me the opportunity to remind you that subscriptions for 1988 are now due, and should be forwarded to the membership secretary.

Yours sincerely

Prudence Harris
SECRETARY

---

Please return to The Secretary City Garden Society 85 Kings Road
London SW5 KR7

Name ..............................Membership No ..............

Address ..........................................................

..................................Postcode......................

I shall/shall not* be attending the AGM on 29 March 1988.

I shall/shall not* require lunch. I enclose a cheque/PO for £5 to cover the cost of the buffet lunch.

Date ........................ Signature ........................

* Please delete as appropriate.

*Example 5.10*

type the headings as you go along. Use A5 paper with the longest edge at the top (landscaped) or A4 with the shortest edge at the top.

The simplest layout is as Example 5.11. Notice that the memo is not signed although sometimes the writer may wish to initial it to show that it has been checked.

You should now be able to type Example 5.11. Set the left-hand margin to line up with the headings then make the right-hand margin slightly narrower, or use margins of 18 and 88 (15 and 70).

You will need to straighten and align your paper for the headings. (See instructions on page 11.) Align your typing line with the bottom of the printed headings. Go to the position of the longest heading (FROM) and tap two spaces before inserting the requisite name. Do the same with REF and DATE.

M E M O R A N D U M

| | | | |
|---|---|---|---|
| FROM | Office Supervisor | REF | OS/GS |
| TO | All Head Office Staff | DATE | 1 September 1988 |

SUBJECT  CHRISTMAS HOLIDAYS 1988

I have heard today that Head Office will be closed in the period between Christmas and New Year. The offices will close at 4.0 pm on Tuesday 24 December and re-open on the morning of Thursday 2 January 1988.

Friday 27 December will be considered as part of the Bank Holiday entitlement but Monday and Tuesday 30 and 31 December will be part of annual leave in accordance with Contracts of Employment.

I wanted to let you all know the dates as soon as they were confirmed so that you could make any necessary arrangements for this holiday period.

*Example 5.11*

## 14 Taking copies and circulation lists

Usually at least one copy of a memo is taken for the file, but when the information must be circulated to a number of people other than the addressee, several copies must be taken. If you read the memo in Example 5.12 you will see why.

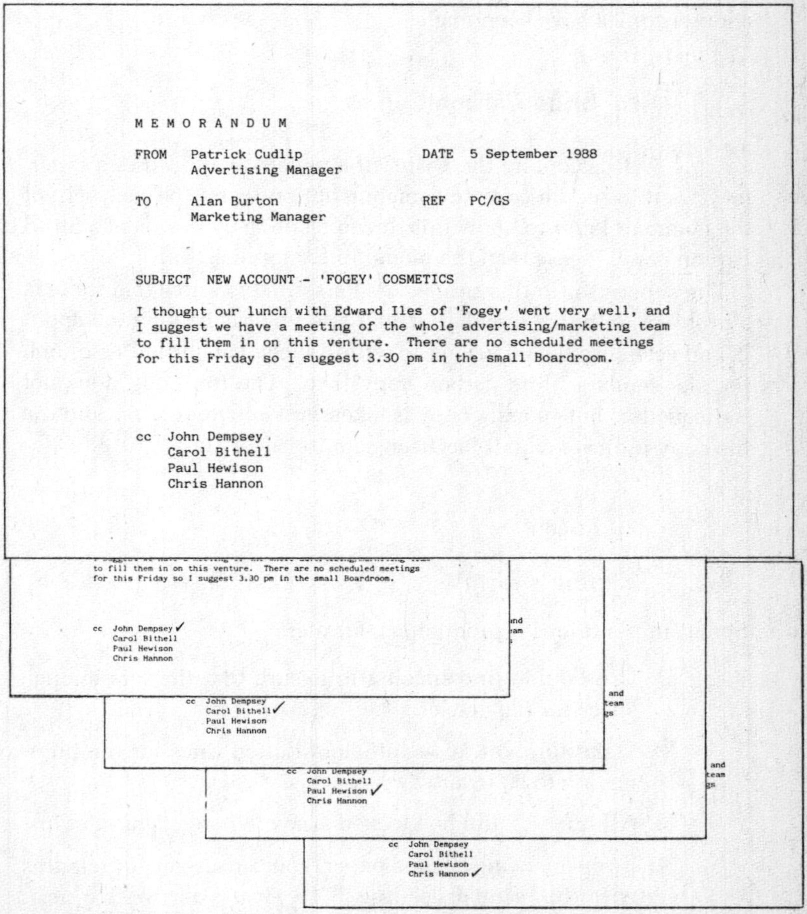

M E M O R A N D U M

FROM Patrick Cudlip DATE 5 September 1988
Advertising Manager

TO Alan Burton REF PC/GS
Marketing Manager

SUBJECT NEW ACCOUNT - 'FOGEY' COSMETICS

I thought our lunch with Edward Iles of 'Fogey' went very well, and I suggest we have a meeting of the whole advertising/marketing team to fill them in on this venture. There are no scheduled meetings for this Friday so I suggest 3.30 pm in the small Boardroom.

cc John Dempsey
Carol Bithell
Paul Hewison
Chris Hannon

*Example 5.12*

cc stands for copy circulated. When Alan Burton receives this memo he knows that the 4 people listed have also had copies informing them of the meeting and isn't left wondering if he needs to tell them or whether Patrick Cudlip will.

Assuming that you want one file copy, you need to take a top copy and 5 carbons. (Or make 5 photocopies.)

After completing the typing tick one name on each copy to indicate who is to receive it. This also serves as a double check that enough copies have been made.

## 15 Blind Carbon Copies

Occasionally the writer of a memo, or indeed of a letter, may want to send a copy to someone but not want the recipient of the memo or letter to know this. It can be done by means of a blind carbon copy. Please read the memo in Example 5.13.

The supervisor in this case wants Personnel to know that there is a problem with this member of staff and what is being done about it, and yet doesn't want to have to write a special memo to Personnel. So, she sends a blind carbon copy (bcc). The top copy does not indicate this, but an extra copy is taken for Personnel. This, and the file copy indicate who it has been sent to. See Example 5.13.

## 16 Forms

### *Typing a form*

Some simple rules for producing a form are:

1. Use double line spacing to ensure that there is enough space for the entries.
2. Make sure you type sufficient dotted lines for the information to be inserted.
3. All lines should be blocked at the left and right margins.
4. If you are using headed paper, you can align your margins with the printed heading. This gives your work a neat, compact appearance.

M E M O R A N D U M

FROM Secretarial Staff Supervisor DATE 31 August 1988

TO Jane Green - Secretary to REF SSS/GS
Alan Burton

SUBJECT LATENESS

Mr Burton has spoken to me about your lateness, both first thing in the morning and when you come back after lunch. I understand that he has already spoken to you personally about this problem. As you know, he is concerned that clients are often unable to reach either him or yourself and cannot then be given the information that they need. Clearly this situation cannot continue.

Perhaps you would come to see me at 9.0 am this Friday 5 September, in my office.

he has already spoken to you personally about this problem. As you know, he is concerned that clients are often unable to reach either him or yourself and cannot then be given the information that they need. Clearly this situation cannot continue.

Perhaps you would come to see me at 9.0 am this Friday 5 September, in my office.

bcc Personnel ✓
fc

ugust 1988

/GS

oth first thing in
I understand that
s problem. As you
le to reach either
rmation that they

Perhaps you would come to see me at 9.0 am this Friday 5 September, in my office.

bcc Personnel
fc ✓

*Example 5.13*

5. Headings should be followed by one or two line spaces before any line for information insertion is typed.
6. The information line can either be typed using the underscore or continuous dots. Points 5 and 6 should be consistent within one document.

Example 5.14 is an attendance sheet for an examination board. Use

SECRETARIAL STUDIES DIPLOMA

Examination Board - 4 July 1983

<u>In attendance</u>

Jane Smythe ..................................

Bryan Watts ..................................

Malcolm Hitchcock ............................

Irene Iles ...................................

Brenda Atchison ..............................

Jennifer Green ...............................

Linda Matthews ...............................

Secretary to Board ...........................

*Example 5.14*

A4 paper and 2 in or 50 mm margins. Leave 2 ins clear at the top of the paper (turn up 13 lines).

Example 5.15 on page 83 is a standard letter. Use A5 paper, suitable equal margins and set your line spacing to 2.

## *Completion of forms*

When you type on dotted or continuous lines you should raise the position of the typing line so that the letters do not touch the lines, otherwise they may be difficult to read.

To do this use either the interliner which releases the platen and allows you to re-align the alignment scale so it is just clear of the line, or use the variable line spacer to do the same thing.

Where you are asked to delete a line as appropriate, the deletion should be made either using lower-case x:

xxxxxx/postal order

or using the hyphen:

cheque/~~postal order~~

Date as Postmark

Dear ___________________________

ACCOUNT NUMBER ______________________

For your information I write to inform you that at

close of banking on _____________________________

your current account was _________________________

overdrawn.

Yours faithfully

Cecil Bradshaw
Branch Manager

*Example 5.15*

Type the form in Example 5.16 on a sheet of A5 landscaped. Use margins of 30 and 70 (25 and 55). Remember to leave space for the postcode.

NAME ......................................

ADDRESS ...................................

...........................................

............... POSTCODE .................

DATE ......................................

*Example 5.16*

Now turn the paper back to the name line. Adjust the typing line and complete the form with your own details. Your work should look like (a) on page 84, with the name just above the dotted line, not like (b) with the name too high, nor like (c).

**a** NAME ..Gill Sugden.......... ✓

**b** NAME Gill Sugden ........................ ✗

**c** NAME ..Gill.Sugden............ ✗

# 6 *Tabulation*

You may need to set out your work in columns, and occasionally to rule it up so that it is enclosed in a box. In this chapter different techniques are gradually incorporated into the examples. There is plenty of additional practice material in Part II.

## 1 The tabulator

A tabulator key enables the typist to move the typing point quickly to a pre-set position rather than tapping across the line of typing. You may be working on an older portable machine that does not have tab keys, or you may have a machine in which they are pre-set. However, the majority of machines will allow the user to set tab stops at any point on the scale.

First, clear any tabs which may be set. You will either have a clear key or a rocker switch marked + and – for set and clear respectively. Locate the tab key which will be separate from this, it may be marked tab or have an arrow → , or on older machines there may be a tab bar at the top of the keyboard. To clear tabs, return to the left margin. Press the tab key, and when the carriage stops press the *clear* or —, the key/switch. Repeat this right across the carriage.

Check in the machine manual to see if this action clears all the tabs at one time, or whether there is a separate key for clearing all the tab stops together.

For practice set tabs at 15, 30, 45, 60. Use the carriage release key to take your typing point to 15 on the scale. Press set or the + key. Repeat this for the other settings. Return the carriage and use the tab key to check that the stops have been set.

If you are using an electric or electronic machine you may have a key which will take you back along the line of typing rather than having to use the carriage return. This is useful with any type of display work.

## 2 Column work

Example 6.1 should be typed on a sheet of A5 paper landscaped, so that there are equal left and right margins and equal top and bottom margins. Follow the instructions below.

SOME COUNTRIES AND THEIR CAPITALS

| | | | |
|---|---|---|---|
| Norway | Oslo | Italy | Rome |
| France | Paris | Greece | Athens |
| Netherlands | The Hague | United Kingdom | London |
| Spain | Madrid | Eire | Dublin |
| Austria | Vienna | Hungary | Budapest |

*Example 6.1*

### *To centre the work horizontally*

1. Find the longest word in each column. This will give you:

   Netherlands The Hague United Kingdom Budapest

   Now decide how many spaces you will leave between each column. Conventionally it is 3, 5, or 7. Five spaces gives a good result under most circumstances.

2. Clear all margins and tab stops. Move your carriage so that the typing point is at 50 (40) on the scale. This will be the centre point of the A5 paper landscaped. (Where machines have a scale with 0 at the centre point, you should use this.)

3. Use the backspace key to backspace *once* for every *two* characters (i.e. letters, symbols or spaces) in the longest line of each column. Remember that 5 spaces are to be left between columns. The first few times you do this it helps to say it aloud. You should backspace once for each group separated by an oblique line, as set out below:

ne / th / er / la / nd /s space / space space / space space / th / e space / ha / gu / e space / space space / space space / un / it / ed / space k / in / gd / om / space space / space space / space b / ud / ap / es / (Ignore any odd letters, in this case the final *t*.)

**4.** To set the tab stops, tap out the number of letters in the longest line of column 1 and 5 spaces for the gap between columns 1 and 2. Set a tab.

Tap out the letters and space of the longest line of column 2 and 5 spaces for the gap between columns 2 and 3. Set a tab.

Repeat for column 3. You do not need to tap out column 4 since no more tab stops are needed.

### *To centre the work vertically*

**5.** Fold the paper loosely from top to bottom and either make a tiny crease or a pencil mark at the middle on one side. Insert the paper into the machine. (Remember that if your scale has 0 as a centre mark you must adjust your paper to be centred around this 0.) Otherwise, your paper should have the left edge at 0 on the scale.

Line up the crease or pencil mark with the alignment scale and take the typing point to the left margin.

Turn the platen knob *anticlockwise* one notch for each line of the tabulation. Thus:

| | |
|---|---|
| Heading | turn one notch |
| Linespace | ,, ,, ,, |
| Norway | ,, ,, ,, |
| France | ,, ,, ,, |
| Netherlands | ,, ,, ,, |
| Spain | ,, ,, ,, |
| Austria | ,, ,, ,, |

At last! Now you are ready to type the table! First type the heading, return carriage twice. Now line by line, **Norway** (press tab key) **Oslo** (press tab key) **Italy** (press tab key) **Rome** carriage return, and complete the table. *The alternative is to make a guess!*

Example 6.2 has column headings and should be worked in the same way. Include the column headings in your calculations when looking for the longest line and when working out where the first line of typing should be. Use A5 paper landscaped.

Example 6.3 is similar. (If you have a Dec Tab (decimal tab) key on your machine, look up your manual for instructions for use.) If your finished table looks like (a) or (b) in Figure 6.1 then you need to look again at point 5 on page 87.

If your work looks like (c) then look again at point 3 on page 86. You are not backspacing correctly.

If your work is like (d) then you need to check on your tapping out for the tab stops and check with point 2 on page 86. You are not putting equal spaces between the columns or not tapping out the longest line in each column.

WEATHER REPORTS FOR 5 SEPTEMBER

| ENGLAND | WEATHER | CANADA AND US | WEATHER |
|---|---|---|---|
| London | Cloudy | Montreal | Rain |
| Birmingham | Rain | New York | Sunny |
| Bristol | Rain | Vancouver | Cloudy |
| Norwich | Cloudy | Chicago | Fair |
| Manchester | Dull | Miami | Fair |
| Newcastle | Dull | Washington | Sunny |
| Carlisle | Rain | | |

*Example 6.2*

FOREIGN EXCHANGE RATES

| Country | Bank Sells | Country | Bank Sells |
|---|---|---|---|
| Austria | 27.00 | Malta | 0.616 |
| Belgium | 78.50 | Netherlands | 4.33 |
| Canada | 1.865 | Norway | 11.33 |
| Denmark | 14.00 | Portugal | 222.00 |
| France | 11.75 | Spain | 222.00 |
| Germany | 3.85 | Sweden | 11.43 |
| Greece | 178.00 | Switzerland | 3.17 |
| Ireland | 1.28 | USA | 1.37 |
| Italy | 2,575.00 | Yugoslavia | 450.00 |

*Example 6.3*

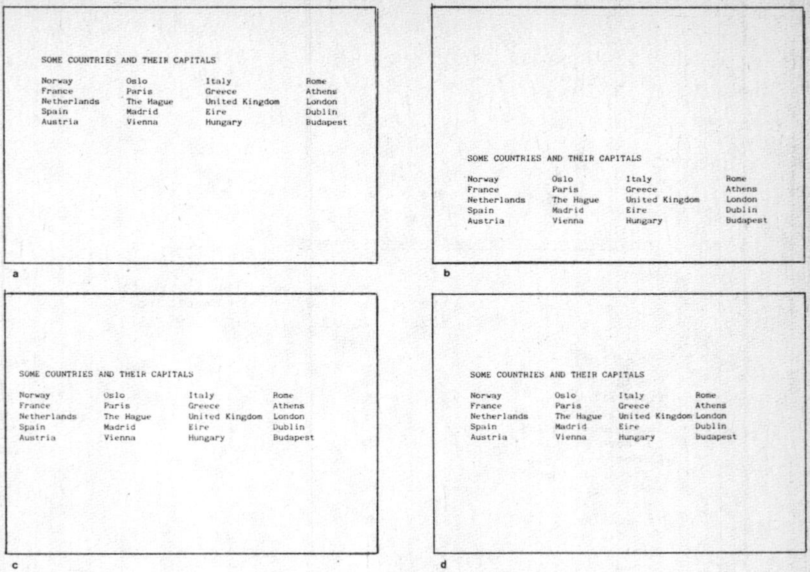

a

SOME COUNTRIES AND THEIR CAPITALS

| | | | |
|---|---|---|---|
| Norway | Oslo | Italy | Rome |
| France | Paris | Greece | Athens |
| Netherlands | The Hague | United Kingdom | London |
| Spain | Madrid | Eire | Dublin |
| Austria | Vienna | Hungary | Budapest |

b

SOME COUNTRIES AND THEIR CAPITALS

| | | | |
|---|---|---|---|
| Norway | Oslo | Italy | Rome |
| France | Paris | Greece | Athens |
| Netherlands | The Hague | United Kingdom | London |
| Spain | Madrid | Eire | Dublin |
| Austria | Vienna | Hungary | Budapest |

c

SOME COUNTRIES AND THEIR CAPITALS

| | | | |
|---|---|---|---|
| Norway | Oslo | Italy | Rome |
| France | Paris | Greece | Athens |
| Netherlands | The Hague | United Kingdom | London |
| Spain | Madrid | Eire | Dublin |
| Austria | Vienna | Hungary | Budapest |

d

SOME COUNTRIES AND THEIR CAPITALS

| | | | |
|---|---|---|---|
| Norway | Oslo | Italy | Rome |
| France | Paris | Greece | Athens |
| Netherlands | The Hague | United Kingdom | London |
| Spain | Madrid | Eire | Dublin |
| Austria | Vienna | Hungary | Budapest |

*Figure 6.1*

All the above examples have main headings. Examples 6.2 and 6.3 also have column headings. In Example 6.2 closed capitals are used for both, while in Example 6.3 the column headings are in lower case with initial capitals and underscore. This choice of layout is a personal preference; you may favour another or have to follow specific instructions. Spaced capitals can also be used for a main heading, as in Example 6.4.

## 3 Longer headings in tables

In Example 6.4 the column headings are long and take up more than one line. Notice that the column headings are wider than the columns, and this should be taken into account when working out the position of the margins and tabs. Also, the headings line up across the bottom.

DEPARTMENT OF INFORMATION STUDIES

Secretarial and Office Studies Student Numbers

| Subject | Year of Course | No of Students enrolled on option | No of Students referred from previous year |
|---|---|---|---|
| Post 'A' Level | | | |
| Shorthand | I | 80 | 12 |
| Typewriting | I | 80 | 4 |
| Transcription | I | 80 | 10 |
| Secretarial Duties | I | 43 | 1 |
| Business Organization | I | 37 | 2 |
| Economic and Financial Aspects | I | 80 | 6 |
| Word Processing | I | 80 | 3 |
| Shorthand | II | 48 | 2 |
| Typewriting | II | 48 | 1 |
| French | II | 48 | 3 |
| Spanish | II | 32 | 1 |
| German | II | 10 | 4 |
| Italian | II | 6 | 0 |
| Information Technology | II | 48 | 7 |
| Postgraduates | | | |
| Shorthand | I | 30 | 2 |
| Typewriting | I | 30 | 0 |
| Transcription | I | 20 | 6 |
| Word Processing | I | 30 | 4 |
| Administrative Practices | I | 30 | 0 |
| Law | I | 12 | 0 |
| Accounting | I | 10 | 3 |
| Business World | I | 8 | 1 |

*Example 6.4*

The method of working is exactly the same as that given for Example 6.1. Since there are 2 main headings you may like to leave an extra line (i.e. 2 clear lines) between them so that they stand out.

Since the numbers do not have to be totalled and have no decimal points, they can be aligned to the left of the column.

Type this on A4 paper. Check the number of characters across the page before beginning.

Note that the subject Economic and Financial Aspects takes up 2 lines: the continuation line has been indented 2 spaces to show this, and the corresponding column entries line up with this continuation line.

## 4 Leader dots

In Example 6.5 there are 3 new points to note: leader dots, a column headed with a £ sign, and typing money in columns.

Leader dots are used to lead the eye across from one column to another, either where for some reason there is a large gap, or as in this case, where the lines are of very unequal length.

When a column is headed by a £ sign treat it as a heading, and block it to the left of the column. When money is presented like this you may align the decimal tab as shown here, but as the columns are not being totalled it is also correct to block each amount of money to the left of the column if you wish. However, I think you will agree

HURRY! WHILE STOCKS LAST!

JEWELLERY SALE

| Item | RRP | Our Price |
|---|---|---|
| | £ | £ |
| 9ct Gold 9 Stone Sapphire & Diamond Cluster ... | 340.00 | 189.00 |
| 9ct Gold Half Wishbone ...................... | 29.60 | 15.99 |
| 9ct Gold Single Stone Diamond ................ | 117.80 | 59.50 |
| 24" 9ct Gold Rope Chain...................... | 80.48 | 42.99 |
| 20" 9ct Gold Rope 70 Chain .................. | 134.60 | 72.40 |
| 9ct Gold Sapphire & Zirconia 7 Stone Cluster .. | 38.80 | 19.99 |
| Pulsar Gents' Quartz Gold-plated case ........ | 30.95 | 25.95 |
| Seiko Gents' Quartz Gold-plated case ......... | 89.50 | 50.50 |
| Silver Plated 4 Piece Tea-set ................ | 57.75 | 29.95 |
| "Wellington" Quartz Carriage Clock ........... | 24.99 | 9.95 |

*Example 6.5*

that an advertisement of this type is more easily read in the style shown. If you follow this, be sure that the first amounts of money to be typed allow for any larger amounts further down the column, otherwise the tab alignment will not work. (See page 91.)

Type Example 6.5 on A4 paper sideways. Use exactly the same method of calculation as before. After working out the tab stops, and setting them, tab across to the column *after* the leader dots. Backspace the number of spaces you have allowed in the table, and then set a tab. When you have typed the table down to the first line with leader dots, work as follows:

Tab across to the *right-hand side* of column 2 and insert a dot. Now take the carriage back to the left-hand margin and type the table in the normal way. Insert the leader dots as you go, leaving one clear space after the last letter of the words in column 2 before putting the first dot.

## 5 Ruling up a table

A table often looks better if it is enclosed in a box. Much of this can be done while the paper is in the typewriter.

If you have an electronic typewriter there may be a key for typing vertical lines – if so, read the manual for use and experiment with Example 6.6. Some machines will produce a vertical line but if it is not possible to make it continuous, you may find it easier to follow the instructions below.

Example 6.6 shows the number of line spaces which should be allowed for vertical position on the paper, and also how you can use the typewriter to help draw up the box.

HOW TO COMPLETE YOUR ORDER FORM

2

| 2<br>1 | Description | Code | Size | Price each<br>£ | Qty | Total value<br>£ |
|---|---|---|---|---|---|---|
| 2<br>1 | Corkscrew | 83Z0 | - | 19.99 | 1 | 19.99 |
| 2<br>1 | Wine Cradle | 95G8 | 1 | 39.99 | 2 | 78.92 |

*Example 6.6*

1. Use A5 paper landscaped. Allow 5 spaces between columns. Position left margin in usual way.
2. Tap across, setting the tab stops, but this time tap out the last column and 1 extra space. Set the right margin at this point.
3. You are now ready to count up the lines that you will use. Turn 1 notch anticlockwise on the platen from the centre point marked with a crease or pencil mark, thus:

| | |
|---|---|
| Heading | one notch |
| Linespace | ,, ,, |
| Linespace | ,, ,, |
| Line | ,, ,, |
| Linespace | |
| Column heading 1st line | ,, ,, |
| Column heading 2nd line | ,, ,, |
| Linespace | ,, ,, |
| Line | ,, ,, |
| Linespace | |

And so on down to the bottom line.

4. Type the heading on the left margin.
5. Return the carriage 3 times. Press the margin-release key and backspace once. Now use the underscore to insert the first ruled line across to the right-hand margin. (If you have an electronic machine, use the repeater key, holding it down until you reach the right-hand margin.) If you have a manual machine try tapping your first fingers alternately on the underscore. You can get up quite a speed that way.
6. Return the carriage once. You are not going to put in guide dots for the vertical lines. These are usually made by disengaging the ribbon so that only an impression is made on the page. If your typewriter uses a ribbon cassette, this should be removed. (If you do not want to do this, the dots will be small enough to be concealed by the ruling.)

Tab across to column 2. Backspace 3 spaces and put a dot.

Tab to column 3. Backspace 3 spaces and put a dot.

Repeat for columns 4, 5, and 6. Put the ribbon back to print.

It is a good idea to put one set of dots near the top of the table and one near the bottom. If you prefer, rule the whole table up after typing it, using a biro pen and ruler.

7. Return the carriage and insert the first line of headings. Then type the second line. Carriage return and insert the next ruled horizontal line. Return the carriage twice. Put in the next line of typing, beginning 'Corkscrew'. Return carriage once.

   Type the next horizontal line. This time return the carriage once and insert another line of guide dots. Return the carriage once.

   Complete the table. Take the paper out of the typewriter and, with the bevelled edge of the ruler down, carefully line up the dots and insert the vertical lines with a biro pen.

   A general rule for typing between horizontal lines is to type the line, return the carriage twice, put in the typing, and then return the carriage *once* before typing the bottom line. This way your work will always be centred between the two lines.

In Example 6.7 you can practise putting horizontal and vertical lines into a table. Leader dots and footnotes are also included. Use A5 paper landscaped.

1. Set your left margin and your tab stops as shown in Example 6.1.
2. Remember to set a right-hand margin as in Example 6.6.
3. In calculating how many lines to use, include each line of typing and all the clear lines.
4. After the first horizontal line put in guide dots for the vertical lines.

Information Technology Adoption and Usage
(44 large organizations 1982/83)

| Technology | Current Usage | Planned Usage |
|---|---|---|
| Mainframe .................... | High* | High |
| Minicomputers ................ | High | High |
| Microcomputers ............... | High | High |
| Data Communication Networks ... | High | High |
| Word Processing .............. | High | High |
| Distributed Computing ........ | Medium | High |
| Facsimile Transfer ........... | Medium | High |
| Viewdata ..................... | Low | Medium |
| Electronic Mail .............. | Low | Medium |
| Teleconferencing ............. | Low | Low |

* High = 70% or more of sample organizations
Medium = 40% to 60% of sample organizations
Low = less than 40% of sample organizations

*Example 6.7*

5. Before typing the line beginning 'Mainframe' insert the right-hand leader dot.
6. Near the bottom of the table put in another line of guide dots.
7. Finally, rule up the vertical lines.

Example 6.8 gives you the opportunity to type a table with multiple headings. Type the table on A5 paper landscaped. Your order of

HOW MUCH DOES IT COST?

| Present Age Male | Present Age Female | £20 Monthly Sum Assured | £20 Monthly Sum + Annual Bonus | £50 Monthly Sum Assured | £50 Monthly Sum + Annual Bonus |
|---|---|---|---|---|---|
| | | £ | £ | £ | £ |
| 18-28 | 18-32 | 2,129 | 3,251 | 5,492 | 8,386 |
| 30 | 34 | 2,128 | 3,249 | 5,489 | 8,382 |
| 35 | 39 | 2,123 | 3,242 | 5,479 | 8,362 |
| 40 | 44 | 2,111 | 3,223 | 5,445 | 8,315 |
| 45 | 49 | 2,089 | 3,190 | 5,388 | 8,227 |
| 50 | 54 | 2,053 | 3,135 | 5,296 | 8,087 |
| 55 | 59 | 1,998 | 3,051 | 5,153 | 7,869 |

*Example 6.8*

working is similar to that given for Example 6.6 but you should not put the guide dots in for the vertical lines until you insert the £ line.

Check carefully before inserting the *second* horizontal line that you have backspaced from the correct tab stop.

*What the finished result should not look like:*

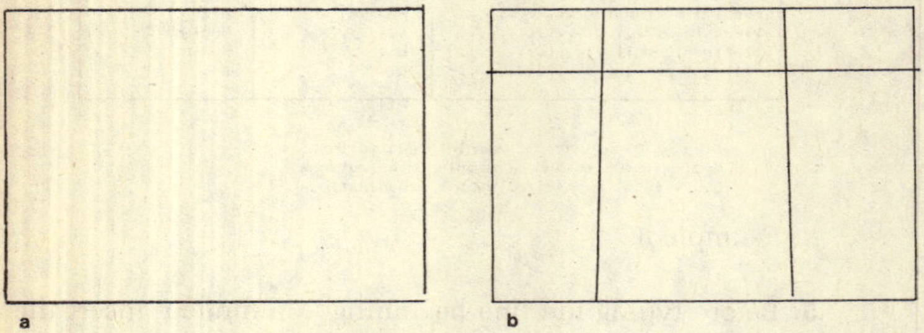


*Figure 6.2*

If your work looks like (a) in Figure 6.2 then there are 3 points to improve upon. Typing pressure should be even right across the horizontal lines. Vertical lines must go from top to bottom and *meet* but not cross the horizontals.

Lastly, patching up of lines must not show. Ensure that you put the tip of the biro on the horizontal line and draw a firm line to touch the next horizontal.

If your work looks like (b) then you are either measuring the space between the columns incorrectly or not putting in the guide dots in a consistent way. Again lines are crossing instead of meeting.

# 7 *Display*

There are occasions when documents need to be displayed in such a way that they have more impact on the reader, for example in the case of notices.

This chapter gives examples of a range of notices with instructions on how to type them as simply as possible and to the best effect.

## 1 Postcards

Postcards can be useful for short messages. Some companies have cards printed with their name and address for this purpose. Others have a range of printed postcards for use in a variety of circumstances, such as acknowledging receipt of an order, or as a reminder. With these types of cards it may only be necessary to type in a few specific details (Example 7.2).

Use a postcard landscaped, with margins of ½ in or 13 mm. Type in double spacing so that you can easily insert numbers and dates and they stand out. By setting narrow margins, you have more space to type in.

Card can be difficult to feed through the machine because of its thickness. A backing sheet will help to keep the card in place if you need to type down to the bottom, but if possible it is better to try to avoid this because you may find that the postcard still slips out of alignment.

The address should go on the front of the card and is typed in the usual way.

If the card looks like the one in Figure 7.1, then try to shorten the message, or type in single or 1½ line spacing.

ST JUDE HOSPITAL   LONDON SW2 3UR

26 July 1986

Our records show that you are now due for your biannual scan, and you are asked to telephone Out-Patients between 1000 and 1600 hours Monday to Friday to make an appointment.

Out-Patients' Record Office

Miss Jane Greenwood
19 Lionel Street
ACTON AC6 2LR

*Example 7.1*

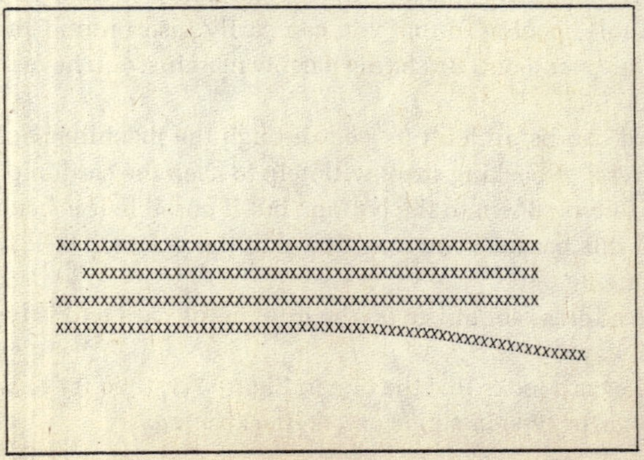

*Figure 7.1*

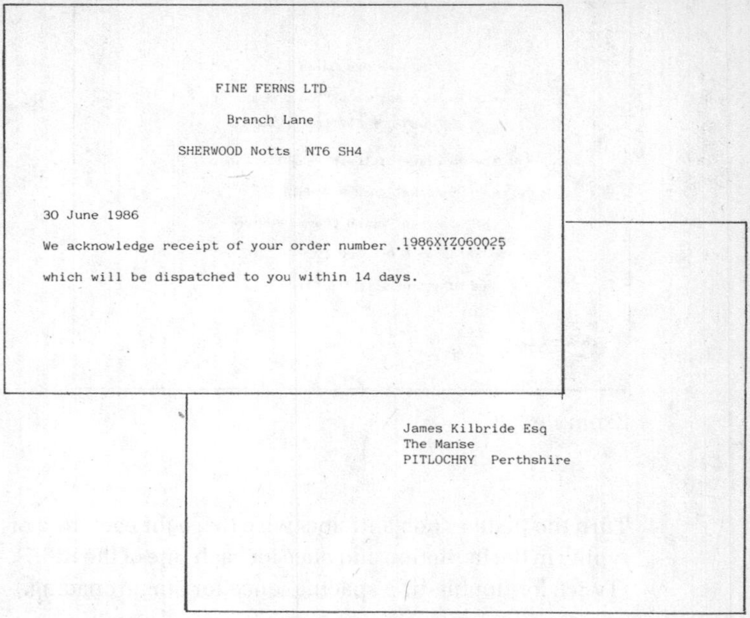
FINE FERNS LTD

Branch Lane

SHERWOOD Notts NT6 SH4

30 June 1986

We acknowledge receipt of your order number .1986XYZ060025

which will be dispatched to you within 14 days.

James Kilbride Esq
The Manse
PITLOCHRY Perthshire

*Example 7.2*

## 2 Invitations

These are generally typed on A6 paper or card, but may be typed on a postcard. The longest side forms the top edge. It is usual to put the wording in the third person, and to type in double spacing.

Invitations are normally sent out in an envelope.

In Example 7.3 each line is centred because it is a formal invitation.

1. Clear the margins.
2. Find where to begin typing by making a pencil mark at the edge, halfway down the paper or card.
3. Insert the paper and line up the pencil mark with the alignment scale.

Mr and Mrs Smith

request the pleasure of the company of

....Vernon & Fiona Black....

at the marriage of their daughter Carole

to Mr James McDonald

at St Agnes Parish Church Merton

on Saturday 6 October 1986 at 2.0 pm

and afterwards at The Grand Hotel

RSVP
10 Acre Lane
Merton

*Example 7.3*

**4.** Turn the platen knob anticlockwise *twice* for each line of typing in the invitation and *once* for each line of the RSVP. (Twice for double-line spacing, once for single spacing.)

**5.** Take the typing point to the centre of the card using carriage release. Use the backspace key to backspace once for every two letters and/or spaces in the first line. Type that line. (The method is the same as that given in point 3, page 86, although no margins are needed this time.)

**6.** Return carriage twice and repeat 5. above for each line of the invitation. Make line 3 – the dotted line – the same length as line 2.

**7.** The RSVP can be positioned ½ in or 13 mm from the left-hand edge and is typed in single spacing.

Example 7.4 is a formally typed acceptance and would be presented in the same way as Example 7.3. However, it is also quite acceptable to write these by hand or buy a printed acceptance card.

Less formal invitations can be typed more simply. In Examples 7.5 and 7.6, follow the instructions given above, from 1 to 4. Repeat point 5 but this time set a margin and begin each line at the left-hand margin. Use the margin release key to override the left-hand margin

Vernon and Fiona Black

thank Mr and Mrs Smith

for the invitation to the marriage of their daughter

Carole

at St Agnes Parish Church  Merton

on 6 October 1986 at 2.0 pm

and have pleasure in accepting

*Example 7.4*

Jane and Michael Blythe

invite you to a dinner to celebrate

the eighteenth birthday of their son

Paul

at Monmouth Grange Hotel, Hastings

on Friday 4 March 1986 at 8.0 pm

RSVP
26 Angel Road
Hastings

*Example 7.5*

and position the RSVP at ½ in or 13 mm. Alternatively, you may set a tab at this point although for one or two lines it is hardly necessary.

In Example 7.6 you will see that there is no RSVP section.

```
Jane and Timothy

invite you to the opening night of their

FRUIT OF THE VINE

Wine Bar

on 12 October from 7.30 pm
```

*Example 7.6*

## 3 Notices and spaced capitals

Notices, as far as typing is concerned, are an extension of typed invitations and the method of working is exactly the same. Each line can be centred, or the longest line centred and a left-hand margin set at the point reached by backspacing.

It may be useful to use spaced capitals on some lines. Take a piece of rough paper and put it in the machine. Take the carriage to the left-hand margin. In closed capitals type:

```
MANCHESTER UNITED
```

Closed means no space between the letters and *one* between the words. Now in spaced capitals type it again:

```
M A N C H E S T E R   U N I T E D
```

Spaced means *one* space after each letter and *three* spaces between words.

Now type Example 7.7(a) and then practise centring in spaced capitals as in Example 7.7(b). Follow the instructions below.

1. Clear the margins. Insert a sheet of A5 paper landscaped and set line spacing at double.

```
MANCHESTER UNITED

M A N C H E S T E R   U N I T E D

LUTON TOWN

L U T O N   T O W N

FEATHERSTONE ROVERS

F E A T H E R S T O N E   R O V E R S

FULHAM FOOTBALL CLUB

F U L H A M   F O O T B A L L   C L U B

SHEFFIELD WEDNESDAY

S H E F F I E L D   W E D N E S D A Y

LONDON WELSH

L O N D O N   W E L S H

QUEENS PARK RANGERS

Q U E E N S   P A R K   R A N G E R S

BRISTOL CITY

B R I S T O L   C I T Y
```

**a**

```
      M A N C H E S T E R   U N I T E D
            L U T O N   T O W N
    F E A T H E R S T O N E   R O V E R S
   F U L H A M   F O O T B A L L   C L U B
    S H E F F I E L D   W E D N E S D A Y
          L O N D O N   W E L S H
    Q U E E N S   P A R K   R A N G E R S
          B R I S T O L   C I T Y
```

**b**

*Example 7.7*

2. Take the typing point to centre of paper.
3. Backspace *once* for each letter and *once* for the space between each word. Type out the line from the point reached. (If you were centring the longest line then you would set a margin at this point.)

Example 7.8(a) has been worked as a fully-blocked notice and Example 7.8(b) a centred one. Try typing both styles. You will see that some decoration has been put in to separate the sections of the notice. These lines must be counted when working out the position of the first line of typing. The method of working is the same as for invitations on pages 99–102.

```
L E A R N   T O   W I N D S U R F

* * * * * * *

RYA TUITION

Local friendly club
with hire facilities
and club shop

* * * * * * *

J O I N   T H E   F U N

SCUDDING SAILBOARDS

THE BEACH HUT
HOVE
```

**a**

**b**

```
        L E A R N   T O   W I N D S U R F

                  * * * * * * *

                   RYA TUITION

               Local friendly club
              with hire facilities
                  and club shop

                  * * * * * * *

             J O I N   T H E   F U N

               SCUDDING SAILBOARDS

                  THE BEACH HUT
                      HOVE
```

*Example 7.8*

Example 7.9 (a) and (b) are menus, and use A5 portrait. Again, try typing both styles. You'll soon discover which is the quickest to produce!

S P E C I A L   M E N U

King of King's Frosted Fruit Cocktail

* * * *

Chef's Special Soup of the Day

* * * *

Roast Turkey
with Festive Trimmings

Savoury Chipolata
and Cranberry Sauce

Brussel Sprouts
and Parsnips

Roast Potatoes

* * * *

Christmas Pudding
Brandy Sauce

* * * *

Mincemeat Delights

* * * *

Coffee

* * * *

**a**

S P E C I A L   M E N U

King of King's Frosted Fruit Cocktail

* * * *

Chef's Special Soup of the Day

* * * *

Roast Turkey
with Festive Trimmings

Savoury Chipolata
and Cranberry Sauce

Brussel Sprouts
and Parsnips

Roast Potatoes

* * * *

Christmas Pudding
Brandy Sauce

* * * *

Mincemeat Delights

* * * *

Coffee

* * * *

**b**

*Example 7.9*

In Example 7.10 the blocked style has been used on A5 landscaped. Here quite a lot of information is being given and it seems clearer to use this style of layout.

```
ARE YOU HARD-WORKING? ? ?

If you are overworked and underpaid

If you would like qualified appointments in your area

If you would like 15% commission

If you want full company backing

If you have a driving licence

AND

If you want to be overworked and overpaid

Then phone us on

02 201 1371 between 1600 and 2000 hours

ANY DAY
```

*Example 7.10*

In Example 7.11 a combination of styles has been used, with the blocked part lined-up with the longest centred line. A5 portrait has been used here.

### 4 Justified right-hand margins

Throughout most of the exercises in this book you have been using a justified left-hand margin, i.e. the left margin has always begun at the same point. You may sometimes want to justify the right-hand side as well.

In Example 7.12, use A5 paper landscaped. When you get to the list of cars, work as follows:

1. Set margins of 1½ in or 38 mm. Also set a tab at the right-hand margin.

Y O U R   L O C A L   N E W S A G E N T

has

IMMEDIATE VACANCIES FOR

DELIVERERS IN

THE FOLLOWING

AREAS

Battersea Rise )
Clapham Road ) SW11
Wandsworth Hill )

CALL HIM ON

955 9955

*Example 7.11*

A S E L E C T I O N

OF

O U R   S E C O N D - H A N D

C A R S

| | |
|---|---|
| New Shape Granada .............................. | £8,995 |
| Ford Granada 2.8 ................................ | £8,499 |
| Sierra 2.0 Ghia ................................. | £4,295 |
| Austin Metro 1.3 HLE ............................ | £3,650 |
| Renault 14 TS ................................... | £2,225 |

C A L L   I N   T O D A Y

To SECOND-HAND SAVERS

*Example 7.12*

2. Tab across to the right-hand margin. Backspace *once* for each character and space in the first line of this column and a further 3 spaces. Insert *one* leader dot, leave 2 spaces, and then type the figures. You will have:

   £8,995

3. Using carriage release go back along the line to the left-hand margin.

4. Type in the first line of the left-hand column, leave 2 spaces and then insert the row of leader dots up to the position of the final one already inserted. You will now have:

   New Shape Granada ........................... £8,995

5. Repeat 2, 3 and 4 above for each subsequent line. (In this particular example all the entries in the right-hand column are the same length, and the leader dots all *end* at the same point. You may therefore see a quicker way of completing the table.)

Example 7.13 is an example of a notice displayed with a justified right margin and no leader dots. In this case there should not be such a wide gap between the left- and right-hand columns, so you need to carefully work out the positions of the margins.

Type Example 7.13 as follows:

1. Work your notice in the usual way, down to the first line with a justified right margin – the one beginning Jane Eyre.

2. Clear the margins and tab stops. Look for the longest line in the left column (For Whom the Bell Tolls), and the longest line in the right column (Ernest Hemingway). Allow 5 spaces between the two columns, as in a tabulation (alternatively, you could allow 3 or 7 spaces.)

3. Take the typing point to the centre of the page and backspace *once* for every *two* characters and/or spaces in this longest line.

   Thus, backspace for each group separated by an oblique line:

These First Editions

ON SPECIAL OFFER

| | |
|---|---|
| Jane Eyre | Charlotte Brontë |
| Wuthering Heights | Emily Brontë |
| Great Expectations | Charles Dickens |
| For Whom the Bell Tolls | Ernest Hemingway |
| Emma | Jane Austen |

for ONE day only

SUNDAY 5 JANUARY

AT

A N T I Q U A R I A N   B O O K S

*Example 7.13*

fo / r space / Wh / om / space / t / he / space B / el / l space / To / ll / s space / space space / space space / Er / ne / st / space H / em / in /gw / ay.

Set the left-hand margin at this point.

4. Tap out the characters and spaces in this line.
5. Set a tab stop. Take the carriage back to the left margin using carriage release key.
6. Type Jane Eyre and go across to the tab setting.
7. Backspace once for each character and space in Charlotte Brontë. Type in Charlotte Brontë. Carriage return twice.
8. Repeat 6 and 7 for each of the lines to be justified. Complete the notice.

## 5 Itineraries and programmes

Tab stops are also useful in work where information is most clearly displayed in column form, for instance in conference programmes and itineraries.

Example 7.14 is a short itinerary. Here it is not necessary to centre the work vertically, although you still want it to look good on the page. As it has 3 columns it is safer to use the A5 paper landscaped, and if you leave 1 in or 25 mm (6 lines) at the top, you will find the position on the paper is quite acceptable.

Type Example 7.14 as follows:

1. Set tabs as shown on page 85.
2. When you have set the margins and tab stops, type in the headings at the top from the left-hand margin.

In Example 7.15 the longest line could be backspaced to set the position of the left-hand margin. Remember to allow for space between the columns.

I T I N E R A R Y

FOR

MR JAMES CROWTHER

| | | |
|---|---|---|
| 12 July | 0950 | Depart Crowther House by car |
| | 1000 | Check-in Concorde Desk - Terminal 1 Heathrow |
| | 1100 | Depart Heathrow flight BA001 for New York |
| | 1000 | Arrive Kennedy Airport - local time |
| | | Car booked for transfer to Waldorf Astoria Hotel |
| Hotel | | |
| 15 July | 1200 | Car booked for transfer to Kennedy Airport |
| | 1300 | Check-in Concorde Desk - Kennedy International |
| | 1400 | Depart Kennedy on flight BA002 for London |
| | 2300 | Arrive Heathrow - local time |
| | | Car to meet arrival and take to Ascot |
| | | Air tickets and confirmation of hotel and car bookings attached |

*Example 7.14*

```
INFORMATION TECHNOLOGY AND THE FUTURE OF MANPOWER

CONFERENCE PROGRAMME

To be held in Main Lecture Theatre
City University

19 March 1987

* * * * * * *

P R O G R A M M E

0930        Opening Remarks
            Chairman - Sir Hugh Blake MBIM

0940        "Careers in Technology"
            James Martin, Research Fellow,
            Institute of Future Technologies

1040        Discussion followed by Coffee Break

1130        "How Far Can We Go With Computers?"
            Professor Madeleine Smith

1225        Discussion followed by Lunch Break

1345        "Technical Training: The Unions' Response"
            David Jacobs, National Training Officer,
            ASTMSIT

1445        Discussion followed by Tea Break

1540        "The Manpower Shortfall"
            Dr Robert Atkinson
            SPRU

1630        Final Discussion
            Concluding Remarks by Sir Hugh Blake

* * * * * * *
```

*Example 7.15*

## 6 Dealing with money

Amounts less than £1 should be shown as follows:

**10p 20p 75p**

There is no space between the amount and p, and no full stop after p.

Whole numbers should be typed as follows:

**£5 £25 £350 £749**

There is no space between £ and the amount.

Either a comma or a space can be used in amounts of a thousand or more. Each of the following is correct:

**£1,000** or **£1 000** **£5,500** or **£5 500**
**£7,000,000** or **£7 000 000** or **£7m**

Sometimes, as in a legal document, figures are followed by the amount in words:

**He was left £200 000 (two hundred thousand pounds).**

When you type a combination of amounts more than or less than £1, be consistent. Type as follows:

**£10.25 £0.15 £26.39 £5.00**

The £ and p sign should never appear together.
**£5.39 £0.39 39p**

Similar rules apply to other currencies:

$5.39 $0.39 *or* **39c**

Type the following for practice:

```
My mother sent me a cheque for £25 (twenty-five pounds).
I saved £5.50 and spent £19.50.
I was given 24p change instead of 38p at the counter.
In 3 pockets I found £2.45, £0.50 and £0.05 respectively.
```

## *Typing columns of money to be totalled*

The methods shown below apply to any figures to be totalled. The simplest layout is blocked style, as shown in Example 7.16(a).

1. £ sign at left of column.
2. Since there are only whole numbers, a decimal point is unnecessary.
3. After typing 1 750, turn the platen knob clockwise 1 notch (½ line spacing). Type underscore the exact width of total column.
4. Turn the platen knob clockwise 3 notches (1½ line spacing) and type in the total.
5. Turn the platen knob clockwise 1 notch and type underscore. Repeat for second line of underscore.

| | | | |
|---|---|---|---|
| **a** £ | **b** £ | **c** £ | **d** £ |
| 380 500 | 99.36 | 99.36 | 99.36 |
| 25 000 | 12.10 | 12.1 | 12.10 |
| 1 750 | 9.75 | 5. | 5.00 |
| | 5.00 | | |
| £407 250 | | £ 116.46 | £116.46 |
| | £126.21 | | |

*Example 7.16*

In Example 7.16(b) there is a decimal point. The method of working is the same as for (a).

Note that the longest line is the total line and the £ at the head of the column should be blocked to the left of the longest line. Make your calculations accordingly.

For the sake of consistency, 2 digits are always inserted after a decimal point.

(c) in Example 7.16 demonstrates some faults: in lines 2 and 3 the digits are not consistent, in the total line there should not be a space after the £ sign and the underscores should not be over or under the £ sign. It should appear as (d).

## *Untotalled columns of money*

Where money does not have to be totalled, the column can be aligned to the right or the left, irrespective of whether the numbers are whole numbers, pence only, or contain decimal points. The £ sign can be inserted before each sum of money rather than at the end of the column. In Example 7.17(a) the columns have been aligned to the right, in (b) they are aligned to the left.

| | | | |
|---|---|---|---|
| **a** | 45p | £98 | £26.31 |
| | 5p | £1 078 | £5.95 |
| | 24p | £326 | £210.50 |
| **b** | 45p | £98 | £26.31 |
| | 5p | £1 078 | £5.95 |
| | 24p | £326 | £210.50 |

*Example 7.17*

This applies in Example 6.3 on page 88. The columns are blocked to the left overall and the same style has been followed within columns 2 and 4.

## 7 Invoices

Whether you have worked in business or not you will be familiar with bills. A bill is, in commercial terms, an invoice for goods purchased. You may pay and take the goods as you usually do in a shop, or you may receive the goods and later get an invoice, as with mail order transactions.

The documents below may all be used in one business transaction; alternatively, just one or two may be used:

Inquiry → quotation → order → advice note → delivery note → invoice → debit note → credit note → statement of account.

The typing style will be very similar in each case. Examples of an invoice and statement of account are given here. They use a range of skills already covered: form completion (page 82), tab setting (page 85), and typing money in columns. First type the invoice shown in Example 7.18.

1. Set a left-hand margin under the Q of Quantity.
2. Set tabs for each column.
3. Depending on the number of items in the invoice, select appropriate line spacing. In Example 7.18 it is double.

   Complete line by line.

Example 7.19 is a Statement of Account and the method of working is the same as above.

I N V O I C E

INVOICE NO 3756

DATE 28 March 1987

Mr and Mrs J Kitney
15 Hollingsworth Drive
POOLE
Dorset PO6 9DR

| QUANTITY | DESCRIPTION | UNIT PRICE | AMOUNT |
|---|---|---|---|
| | | £ | £ |
| 1 | Air Filter | 4.95 | 4.95 |
| 1 | Oil filter | 4.20 | 4.20 |
| 4 | Plugs | 1.18 | 4.72 |
| 1 | Set Points | 1.52 | 1.52 |
| 2 | Headlight Bulbs | 0.42 | 0.84 |
| 1 | Set Front Brake Pads | 9.30 | 9.30 |
| 1 | Sump Washer | 0.12 | 0.12 |
| 1 | Brake Cleaner | 2.20 | 2.20 |
| | Engine Oil - 1 gallon | 5.43 | 5.43 |
| | Total Goods | | 33.28 |
| | Total VAT @ 15% | | 4.92 |
| | TOTAL AMOUNT DUE | | £38.20 |

*Example 7.18*

S T A T E M E N T

STATEMENT 2

DATE 31 October 1987

Mrs G Pickering
192 Haarlem Road
PUTNEY VALE
SW15 4VW

| DATE | ITEM | DEBIT | CREDIT | BALANCE |
|---|---|---|---|---|
| | | £ | £ | £ |
| 0/10/87 | Balance from previous statement | | | 0.00 |
| 10/10/87 | Black Patent Belt | 4.98 | | 4.98 |
| 22/10/87 | White Towel Holder | 2.99 | | 7.97 |
| 28/10/87 | Denim Dungarees | 18.99 | | 26.96 |
| 28/10/87 | Returns | | 4.98 | 21.98 |

*Example 7.19*

# 8 *Running Meetings*

There is a series of documents associated with the running of meetings. The Secretary of an association or committee, or Company Secretary in a large organization, has the responsibility for seeing that the documents are circulated and that correct records are kept.

By working through the sequence of documents in this chapter you should be able to organize and record a meeting and to keep adequate records.

## 1 Notice of meeting

This should be circulated to all those entitled to attend well in advance of the actual meeting date. Sometimes it is circulated as a combined document with the Agenda.

A Notice must contain the name of the body running the meetings, the type of meeting, date, time, place and, finally, the name and designation of the sender.

If a Notice alone is typed then A5 landscaped is probably the most suitable size of paper.

In Example 8.1 centre the longest line in order to get the position of the left-hand margin if you want to be exact. In practice you would probably just make a guess at where to place it.

## 2 Agenda

This lists the topics for discussion at a meeting as well as the order in which they will be discussed. If it is sent out to members of a committee it may well have accompanying documents. (See Item 5 of Example 8.2.)

B I G T O N   S A I L I N G   C L U B

Dock Road   BIGTON-ON-SEA   Somerset

A meeting of the Offshore Committee will be held in the Clubhouse at the above address on Wednesday 23 January 1986 at 8.0 pm.

James Longfellow
Secretary

*Example 8.1*

The first 3 items in Example 8.2 are fairly standard in Agendas, as are the last 2 items.

Again, A5 paper, either portrait or landscaped, is usually large enough unless you have a very lengthy Agenda.

Sometimes a slightly different Agenda is prepared for the Chairman (see Example 8.4).

## 3 Combined Notice and Agenda

The Notice of Meeting and Agenda are frequently sent out together as one document, as in Example 8.3. This document has a more formal tone than previous ones since it is for the AGM of a limited company. You will see that the standard items mentioned above are omitted. This example would be typed on A4 paper, with equal margins.

This type of Notice and Agenda would be sent to all shareholders

BIGTON SAILING CLUB

Dock Road BIGTON-ON-SEA Somerset

Meeting of the Offshore Committee on 23 January 1986
at 8.0 pm.

AGENDA

1 Apologies for absence.

2 Minutes of last meeting.

3 Matters arising from the Minutes.

4 Racing plans for Easter weekend - Commodore to report.

5 Purchase of new boat for 1986 season. (Document A)

6 Preparation of Report for AGM.

7 Any Other Business.

8 Date of next meeting.

James Longfellow
Secretary

*Example 8.2*

in the company. They would also receive a voting form to enable them to vote 'by proxy' if they cannot attend themselves. The person named on this form does not necessarily have to be another shareholder.

## 4 Preparing for a meeting

Preparing for a meeting is the job of the Secretary to the group or committee that is to meet.

SOUTHERN TIMBER PLC

TIMBERYARDS

WOODBRIDGE

SUSSEX

NOTICE IS HEREBY GIVEN that the Second ANNUAL GENERAL MEETING of the Company will be held in the Central Hall High Street Brighton on Monday 19 June 1986 at 1400 hours.

AGENDA

1 To receive the Directors' Report and Statement of Accounts for the year ended 31 March 1986.

2 To declare a dividend.

3 To elect 2 Directors.

On retirement Mr J Blake and Mr A Keats offer themselves for re-election.

4 To re-appoint Moore, Greenwood & Co as Auditors for the coming year.

5 Transaction of Any Other Business.

BY ORDER OF THE BOARD

Brian Worthing
Secretary

28 February 1986

*Example 8.3*

1. There should be spare copies of the Minutes of last meeting and the Agenda.
2. A Chairman's Agenda similar to Example 8.4 which relates to the Agenda on page 119 may need to be prepared. Space is left on the right of the page for the Chairman to make notes. Mention is also made under each item of letters received, and these should be attached to the Agenda for the Chairman.
3. See that there is adequate space in the room, arrange chairs as necessary, provide spare paper and pencils, and glasses and water if the meeting is to last a long time.
4. At a meeting of a non-social group it may be necessary to have past sets of Minutes available for reference.
5. After the meeting all papers etc. should be collected. The

B I G T O N   S A I L I N G   C L U B

Meeting of the Offshore Committee on 23 January 1986 at 8.0 pm.

CHAIRMAN'S AGENDA

NOTES

1 Apologies for Absence.

Letter from John McIntyre, on business in US.

2 Minutes of last meeting.

3 Matters arising from Minutes.

2 letters about organization of Cherbourg Race prior to start.

4 Racing plans for Easter weekend.

Commodore/Chairman to report. Timing list attached.

5 Purchase of new boat for 1986 season.

Document A. Also 6 quotations with details of discounts.

6 Preparation of Report for AGM.

7 Any Other Business.

8 Date of next meeting.

24 February provisional suggestion.

James Longfellow
Secretary

*Example 8.4*

The Sixteenth Meeting of the Offshore Committee of Bigton Sailing Club was held in the Clubhouse on 23 January 1986 at 8.0 pm.

| | | |
|---|---|---|
| PRESENT | John Aspin | (Chairman) |
| | Rosemary White | |
| | Michael Newman | |
| | Gareth Iles | |
| | James Longfellow | (Secretary) |

| | | | ACTION |
|---|---|---|---|
| 1 | APOLOGIES FOR ABSENCE | John McIntyre was on business in US. William Jones was ill. | |
| 2 | MINUTES OF LAST MEETING | These had been circulated with Agenda and were taken as read and signed by Chairman. | |
| 3 | MATTERS ARISING | The Chairman read out 2 letters received from members expressing concern at the confusion over the time of the delayed start in the Cherbourg race. This confirmed the concern felt by the Committee at the last meeting. After discussion it was AGREED that the Squadron Club should be approached to see if a section of notice board could be clearly headed and used in their Clubhouse for that particular weekend in 1986. | RW |
| 4 | RACING PLANS FOR EASTER WEEKEND | The Chairman read out the times and handicaps for the races. These were based on the successful meeting in 1985. In his capacity as Commodore the Chairman told the meeting that this was, he believed, the last year when no charge for organ-ization could be made to members and the Committee were asked to consider how charges might be made to members without a drop in entrants. | |
| | | Details of the Easter Weekend races to be circulated to all members together with catering arrangements. | GI |
| 5 | PURCHASE OF NEW BOAT FOR 1986 SEASON | The Chairman read out the letters received from the short-list of boatbuilders drawn up at last meeting. | |
| | | After discussion it was RESOLVED to place an order for a Westerly 106. Delivery was guaranteed for 31 March 1986 and a 10% discount was available for club purchases. | |

*Example 8.5*

| | | |
|---|---|---|
| 6 PREPARATION OF REPORT FOR AGM | The Secretary listed the main points to be included in the report from the Offshore Committee and members were asked to put in writing any additional points they felt it necessary to report. | |
| 7 ANY OTHER BUSINESS | a) MN raised the problem of catering in the Clubhouse for the Laying-Up Supper because of the numbers now attending. AGREED that some quotations would be sought from local firms. | MN |
| | b) JL expressed concern over rising cost of duplication of notices and minutes and circulation to members. Suggestion that it might be possible to organize delivery by hand. A breakdown of the alternatives available to be carried out prior to next meeting. | JL |
| 8 DATE OF NEXT MEETING | 24 February at 8.0 pm in the Clubhouse. | |

Chairman ...............................

Date ..................................

draft Minutes should be compiled as quickly as possible and sent to the Chairman for approval prior to being circulated to members.

### 5 The meeting

At a meeting it is the job of the Secretary to ensure that any documents which may be needed, together with any correspondence received, are available. The Secretary should take notes on the proceedings and ensure that those attending sign an attendance sheet or book. If it is a big meeting it is usual to list the Committee and then give the number of other people attending.

### 6 Minutes of meetings

These should be typed in reported speech. The order of the Agenda should be followed exactly.

Sometimes a Minute Book is kept and the meetings numbered as follows: 'The sixth meeting of the Offshore Committee of Bigton Sailing Club . . .'

Each Minute of a meeting may be numbered consecutively. The sixth meeting of the Offshore Committee may be numbered 6.1, or follow on from the number used at the fifth meeting. Consecutive numbering makes it easy to refer back to points raised and decisions taken at previous meetings over a period of time.

When there are points to be followed up between meetings it can be useful to have an action column on the right-hand margin, in which can be inserted the initials of the person responsible for carrying out that action (see Example 8.5).

Decisions taken by the meeting should be clearly reported, perhaps by using capitals (see point 5 in Example 8.5).

The layout of Example 8.5 is of the simplest. Use at least a 1 in or 25 mm margin, wider if the Minutes have to be inserted into a file. To position the side headings and their numbers, you can set a tab to the left of the left-hand margin. To insert the number, hold down the margin release key at the same time as you return the carriage, then press tab to reach the position for the next number.

A space is left for the Chairman to sign the Minutes. This will be done at the next meeting (24 February), under Item 2 on the Agenda, if they are agreed to be correct.

# 9 *Addenda*

## 1 Footnotes

Footnotes should be fitted at the bottom of the page. Numbers or symbols can be used. It is essential to estimate the amount of space you need to allow at the bottom of the page and make a pencil mark. Remember to allow room for the bottom margin. See Example 9.1.

```
xxxxxxxxxxxxxxxxxx*   xxxxxxxxxxxxxxxxxxxxxxxxxxxxxxxxxxxxxxx
                                            I
xxxxxxxxxxxxxxxxxxxxxxxxxxxxxxxxxxxxxxxxxxxx   xxxxxxxxxxxxxxx
xxxxxxxxxxxxxxxxxxxxxxxxxx
______________________________________________________________

*    This is a footnote explanation.
I
     This is a footnote symbol. It is typed ½ line above
     the script both here and in the text.
```

*Figure 9.1*

## 2 Reports

A short report, whether formal or informal, will often be presented in the form of a memorandum with a subject heading. It should be in single spacing and have numbered and headed sections with numbered sub-sections and shoulder headings. A formal report should be in the 3rd person. Both types of report should be signed.

Figure 9.2 shows the layout of an informal report.

TO

FROM

Ref

DATE

REPORT ON ____________________

1.0 INTRODUCTION

This contains the terms of reference, the name of the person by whom the report is authorized, the deadline date, and whether or not recommendations are required.

2.0 INFORMATION

2.1 This section contains the findings of the report, and within each of the sub-sections there may be an analysis of the particular problem or situation.

3.0 CONCLUSIONS

This may also contain recommendations if they are required, for example:

I should like to recommend the following action be taken

3.1 ______________

3.2 ______________

3.3 ______________

SIGNATURE

*Figure 9.2*

In a more formal report the sections might be as in Figure 9.3.

1.0 TERMS OF REFERENCE

2.0 PROCEDURE (i.e. the method of obtaining the information)

3.0 FINDINGS (similar to the Information section 2.0 above)

4.0 CONCLUSIONS (it is important <u>not</u> to introduce new evidence in this section)

5.0 RECOMMENDATIONS

*Figure 9.3*

## 3 Manuscript correction signs

The signs shown in Figure 9.4 are used in editing typescript and handwritten documents. The correction sign appears in the margin of the text and a mark is made at the appropriate point in the text. Sometimes there is no marginal instruction, simply a mark in the text. Some of the practice material which follows includes manuscript correction signs.

| *Instruction* | *Marginal mark* | *Textual mark* |
|---|---|---|
| Change marked letters to lower case | lc | Television |
| Change marked letters to upper case | uc | thursday |
| Transpose letters or phrase | trs | thier, there and here |
| Start a new paragraph | NP | // [ |
| Put in a space | # | wehave |
| Close up. Take out space between characters or words | ⁀ | run ning week day |
| Insert character | ⅄ | togeher (t) |
| Let it stand | stet ⊘ | ~~tomorrow~~ |
| Delete | ♂ | leave out |
| Word written out in dotted box where unclear in text | ZIMBABWE | Zimbabwe |
| Run on. No new paragraph | run on | |
| Insert a hyphen | H | cul de-sac |
| Insert a dash | \|-\| | 25 December Christmas Day |

# *Practice Material*

The following pages contain a range of practice material to consolidate the work introduced in the first part of the book.

First, there are a number of copy typing passages to allow you to improve your speed and accuracy. These passages have a stroke count at the end of each line to enable you to work out your exact speed over a given period of time. The method for assessing speed and accuracy is given on pages 45–6.

The majority of the exercises are handwritten and some include the manuscript correction signs described on page 128. The material may be worked through in any order, not necessarily that given.

Recommended solutions for each exercise are provided at the end of this section, with additional notes as necessary. These are not the only acceptable layouts and you may prefer other solutions. Remember to be consistent in style within each piece of work.

## Speed and/or Accuracy Development Exercises

```
It is important to clean your typewriter regularly, not to     62
let rubber dust and paint clog the machine, and to cover it   122
when it is not being used. (28 words)                         143
```

```
In December we begin to panic because often we have not       62
bought our Christmas cards and we find we have already       125
missed the last posting dates to places overseas. (32 words) 158
```

```
You are only going to improve your typing speed now if you     55
concentrate on making your fingers work faster.  This may     115
mean a few more errors but as you get used to the higher      171
working speed your accuracy will gradually improve again.     228
(45 words)
```

Winter is a good time to decide to teach yourself a new 60
skill such as typing because you can sit inside in the 118
warmth and forget about the rain and the short days. (32 words) 159

By the time summer comes and you are out playing tennis or 57
cricket, or swimming regularly, you will also be a 117
proficient typist. (24 words) 124

When you are ill and need to stay away from your job it is 58
usual to telephone your place of work to explain why you 115
will be absent. (26 words) 130

Bank Holidays in England are spread unevenly through the 62
year. By the time Christmas and Easter arrive everyone is 124
exhausted, but in the period from April to August there are 187
four Public Holidays. (39 words) 196

In order to reward excellence and achievement in British 65
industry the Queen's Awards are made annually. (20 words) 102

Many aspects of life in the United Kingdom are getting more 62
and more like the United States: for example, hypermarkets 122
on the edge of urban areas are now a fairly common sight; 182
also it is possible to buy goods on sale throughout most of 232
the year. (46 words)

A good typist must not only know how to type but be able to 58
spot spelling errors, punctuate text, and be aware of the 121
proper use of the many special characters which appear on 185
the typewriter keyboard. (39 words) 194

When one watches an individual performing a skill well, one 62
is generally impressed by the ease with which that skill is 131
carried out. (23 words)

A skilled performance is based on practice. When you first 58
begin to drive a car, depressing the clutch, getting into 120
gear, checking the mirror and moving off from the curb are 176
all major operations: eventually, however, you can manage 234
each movement with some fluency and have time to think about 293
the traffic and the pedestrians as well. It's a matter of 347
practice. (71 words) 356

Nowadays it is easy to do your shopping without going 61
outside your own front door. First of all you have to send 122

off for a catalogue and then you can spend a few minutes or 182
many hours looking through the coloured pages until you have 239
decided which things you are going to buy. It can be almost 300
anything for the home, from electrical appliances through to 360
wallpaper and furnishing materials. You can also order 418
clothes and jewellery, or plants and shrubs for the garden. 479
Once the order form has been completed and put in the post 531
it is a matter of waiting for the door bell to ring and the 590
postman delivering the parcels. If you decide to keep the 649
goods you will, of course, have to pay for them. (137 words) 687

If you make errors when you are typing there are a number of 60
ways that these can be corrected: whichever method you 121
choose the erasure should not be detectable. Always move 184
the carriage to the extreme left or right if using a rubber 241
or liquid. This ensures that dust does not collect round 314
the daisy wheel or in the type basket, and liquid does not 378
get into any part of the machine. However, many new 438
electronic machines today have self-correcting ribbons so 487
that the modern typist does not have to take all these 538
irksome precautions when correcting typing errors. (109 words) 563

Apart from using mail order companies as a means of 51
purchasing clothes, an increasing number of people are going 111
to second-hand or nearly new shops. Many of these are run 169
to collect funds for a specific charity and may be quite 225
particular about the clothes which they are prepared to 280
accept for sale. When this is the case it is possible to 337
find quite expensive clothes and shoes on sale for a small 395
proportion of their original cost. Perhaps the purchaser 452
wore the outfit once or twice or did not even wear it at all 512
because they did not like it when they had taken it home. 569
For whatever reason the clothes are in the shop it is 622
relatively easy to purchase some extremely good bargains. 677
(135 words)

Would you please deliver to the porter at the main desk of 58

our building four dozen ribbons for the electronic 108

typewriters you supplied to us at the end of May. We shall 167

also require six dozen self-correcting ribbons for the same 226

machines. If at all possible we would like to take delivery 286

during this week. (61 words) 304

Mechanized mail handling is one of the most important 54

changes that the Post Office has introduced since the advent 115

of the postage stamp. It will help the move away from the 174
traditional methods of sorting by hand which are very labour 235
intensive. However, to be successful the general public 292
must be educated to use their postcodes. Perhaps if the 349
Post Office succeed, this will be a means of keeping the 406
cost of postage down in the future. (90 words) 448

Some people have a craze for collecting things: other people 60
develop this interest when items of value are left to them 118
by relatives. People collect all sorts of things, such as 176
stamps, coins, pictures, silver, jewellery, jugs, china 231
ornaments, books, matchboxes, cigarette cards. Whatever it 290
is, it may provide the collector with an overriding interest 350
away from his or her place of work and over a period of time 410
that person may well become a recognized expert, sometimes 468
winning international renown. (99 words) 497

Most of us like to plan our holidays well in advance, 53
because one of the nicest things about them is the 103
anticipation during the winter of the bliss of being in the 162
sunshine under a blue sky. It is not always necessary to go 222
to the Mediterranean in order to enjoy this, since many 277
places in central Europe are able to offer the same type of 336
weather, but during winter. Winter sports holidays are 391
becoming increasingly popular because they allow people a 448
break from the rainy and dull skies of Britain just at the 506
time when they need it most. (109 words) 546

## Exercises with corrections and copy exercises

**No. 1** Make the amendments shown in the following passage. Type it in double spacing with margins of 1½ in and 1 in or 38 mm and 25 mm. Use blocked paragraphs.

stet ~~ships~~ boats It seems to have become the vogue to build replicas of ships used on voyages of discovery several 100 years ago, and then to try to sail them along the same routes to their original landfalls. The latest attempt to reenact such a voyage is with a replica of The Golden Hind the boat Sir Francis Drake sailed to St Tohmas in the Virgin Islands. However, the ship had run aground on a midbank at the mouth of the River Avon, and the ships cat had deserted. No further problems were anitcipated on the seven week voyage once she had been refloated and had sailed away.

(after only 24 hours,)

**No. 2** Type the following passage in double spacing with indented paragraphs. Use suitable equal margins.

It is really difficult to make up your mind when you want to buy a microcomputer. There are a bewildering number of ~~things~~ points to be considered. The first ~~consideration~~ of these is whether you need a computer at all and what will you use it for. Once you have established a need do you choose the hardware or the software? Apparently, the latter. When you know what you want to do on the machine you look for the software that best suits ~~your~~ these needs and that you find most user friendly. Having made that decision you then look for the hardware on which to run the programs. Don't think that ends the decision making, however, because you will probably also need a printer. The choice is usually between dot-matrix, NLQ daisywheel or thermal, depending on the speed and quality you require.

What about the price? Probably the best idea is to have an upper limit in mind and to discount software, machinery and printers which exceed this amount as you go through the various sages of making up your mind.

(near letter quality),

**No. 3** Type with indented paragraphs and even margins in 1½ line spacing. Make the amendments as shown.

Making Corrections (Caps) (Centred)

Some attempt has been made to ~~decide on~~ estimate the
ease of correcting mistakes ~~in typed~~ in text when you
the typist does not have a self/correcting element ⅄H
STET in ~~the~~ the keyboard. ~~Points~~ Factors which need to be considered STET
are ~~these~~ the ease of application, how well the mistake is
(with fluids) covered, how quickly the product dri~~ed~~es, and the
ease with which one can type over the correction.
of uc ~~Additionally~~, there is/the problem with a liquid of ⅄also
how quickly it thickens. Some makes seem to
STET thicken ~~quite~~ up. ~~rapidly~~ very fast and ~~so~~ as most of them come
⅄H in narrow/necked bottles, they get 'gunged' up (GUNGED)
and ⸺ the brush won't come out easily. Over
a period of time the resulting waste can become
quite costly.

NP [Coated paper strips are less ~~dirty~~ messy and can be
bought either in a colour to match the paper/used ⅄being
or as a plastic film for use with carbon ribbons.

NP [Both fluid and coated paper are useful
depending on the type of correction being made
and its position on the paper. Still, for ease of
of use, and ~~for~~ speed, the paper/coated strips trs
are probably/The most popular as well as the cheapest
method to use.

**No. 4** Type this notice on a sheet of A5 paper, portrait style.

Spaced Caps

Parewell [ Landscapes (Spaced Caps)

Tarmacking — (Caps)

Crazy paving

Ornamental Walls — (Caps)

Stone Fireplaces

Grass cutting — (caps)

(LOPPING) Tree lopping

We are a reliable Co. and can

caps — guarantee our Clients a

First Class Job ! — (Spaced caps + U/score)

Estimates Free — (Caps)

121 London Road

EPSOM Surrey

(Typist – insert some decoration to separate the sections please)

Phone Today (Caps)

**No. 5** Type the following in four columns on A5 paper landscaped.

← Some Towns

| | | |
|---|---|---|
| Alton | Birmingham | Rotheram |
| Alnwick | Belfast | Rochester |
| Accrington | Bradford | Rotherhithe |
| Ashford | Bournemouth | Runcorn |
| Appledore | Barnstaple | Ripon |

(APPLEDORE)

Salford
Southampton
Sunderland
Swansea
Salisbury

**No. 6** Type this table on A5 paper. Do not rule the table.

Cross-Channel passenger Traffic — caps

| | (in million passengers p.a.) | | |
|---|---|---|---|
| | 1980 Actual | 2000 Projected | % growth p.a. 1980 - 2000 |
| Total Foot passengers | 9.0 | 19.4 | 3.9 |
| Total Sea passengers | 18.2 | 44.9 | 4.6 |
| Air passengers | 2.4 | 3.5 | 1.9 |
| caps. Total passengers* | 20.6 | 48.4 | 4.4 |

* Total cross-Channel passenger traffic to Belgium grew by nearly 3% p.a. between 1970 and 1980.

**No. 7** Type the following information on A5 paper as indicated. Head it DIVISION OF WORDS.

| | Column |
|---|---|
| complacent | 2a |
| atmosphere | 3a |
| examination | 2d |
| relevant | 1c |
| typewriter | 3d |
| satisfaction | 1b |
| preference | 2b |
| agriculture | 3b |
| procedure | 1a |
| recognition | 3c |
| government | 2c |
| friendship | 1d |

please rule up the 3 columns

All of these words can easily be divided if they come towards the end of a line of typing.

NB You should ensure that any typing in conjunction with a table should not extend beyond the margins of that table.

**No. 8** Type the following information and rule up the table.

Schedule of Travelling Time caps.

| | Total Time | | Walking/Waiting Time | |
|---|---|---|---|---|
| | hrs. | mins. | hrs. | mins. |
| London Paris air | 4 | 25 | 1 | 45 |
| London Paris sea | 7 | 25 | 1 | 10 |
| London Brussels air | 4 | 00 | 1 | 45 |
| " " sea | 7 | 45 | 1 | 10 |

**No. 9** Type the table as given below on A5 paper.

| Employment Type | Employment Created | |
|---|---|---|
| | Direct | Indirect |
| Construction workers | 800 - 1000 | 1200 - 1500 |
| Electricians | 2000 - 3000 | 2600 - 4000 |
| Carpenters and Joiners | 3500 - 5000 | 6000 - 8000 |

The Title is JOB CREATION - THE CHANNEL FIXED LINK.

**No. 10** Type this table on A4 paper.

WOMEN MANAGERS AS A PERCENTAGE OF TOTAL – 1979

| Managerial Group. | % managers who are women |
|---|---|
| General management | Not available |
| Managerial | |
| Production, works + maintence | 20.3 |
| Managers and Works Foreman (a→e) | 4.6 |
| Site and other managers | 2.9 |
| Transport Managers | 3.4 |
| Managers in warehousing and materials handling | 2.9 |
| Office Managers. | 19.1 |
| managers in wholesale and retail distribution | 30.4 |
| Publicans, Restaurauteurs and Club Stewards | 41.6 |
| All managers, but exluding those in office(s) | |
| Wholesale + retail distribution, Publicans Restaurauteurs and Club Stewards | 10.1 |

Indent 2 spaces from margin

Indent

Source EC Labour Force Survey 1979.

**No. 11** Type this letter on A4 paper and take a carbon copy.

Our Ref. JB/CA19 Dated 1/11/88

To

Mrs J Blythe

80 Langley Road

Berkhampstead Herts

BK6 HEY

Dear Mrs B

Account No 19860437

I'm writing in reply to yr letter of last Thursday to inform y that we have paid the 2 cheques for

H £307 + £550 into yr above named account.

We have, at the same time, transferred £1000 to yr deposit account as requested. The balance remaining on yr current account as at close of business yesterday was £842.

Yours sincerely

BERKHAMPSTEAD BANK

John Smiley

Manager.

**No. 12** Type this letter on A4 paper. You may be able to fit it on one side but if not, use a continuation sheet.

Our Ref. RR/85RW

2 NOV. 88

R. Reardon Esq.

97 London Road

Blackheath - caps. London SE3 6BL

Dear Mr R

I have pleasure in writing with final details of the arrangements we have made for you, your wife, and

STET your 2 ~~children~~ daughters Elizabeth and Heather ~~[illegible]~~ (Typist put Nos of paragraphs in left margin)

1 19 June ~~86~~ '88 Heathrow to Singapore

29 June " onward flight Singapore to Hong Kong

4 July " " " H.K. to ~~Katmandu~~ Kathmandu

9 " " Return " Kathmandu TO Heathrow London

2 Hotel accomodation of 2 (two) double rooms each with private bath at

Luxor Palace, Singapore

Holiday Inn, H K

Imperial Palace Hotel, Kath.

4 I enclose details of the various ~~trips~~ excursions and short walking tours that can be made in Kath.

cont.

Should any be of interest to you it may be poss. to make reservations prior to yr. departure.

5 I also enclose partics. of the two personal/ medical/ baggage insurance schemes we offer. When you have decided on the one you wish to take out for you and your family perhaps you ~~will~~ would return the completed Proposal Form to me.

3 Arrangements with Asiacar for a small self-drive car to be ~~waite~~ waiting at the hotels in Singapore and H.K. on yr arrival. Keys will be at reception.

I hope these arrangements meet with your wishes, and lk forward to hearing from you shortly.

Yours Sinc.
FAR EAST TRAVEL CO.

James Browne
Personal Tours Man.

**No. 13** Type a memo to Accounts Department from Sales Manager; date 9/3/88, ref AD/GS. Use a form.

Re: Jameson Bros.

Would you please note that the above account holders have
lc exceeded their Credit Limit. ~~but~~ We have made
some investigations and understand that the Co
d are in some financial difficulty ~~(euphemism)~~. Therefore,
no further orders should be accepted from them
lc until their account is brought back within the Limit as
NP set. [Wld you please see that all members of your
sales staff receive this information.

cc Managing Dir.
Marketing Man.

**No. 14** Type the following memo.

To Dean's Sec. 15/7/88
From All members of Staff (NB Except Travolta!) AS/GS

d I'm sure that by now you ~~all~~ know that
the Porter George Travolta is retiring at the
uc end of this term after being with the college
for almost fifteen years.

Anyone who would like to contribute to a
leaving present for George is asked to bring their money
to my office before 20 July. There will be a presentation
uc by the dean at the end of term staff meeting
on 21st July.

**No. 15** Set out suitably.

Memorandum

From Personnel manager 15/12/88

To all Departmental Heads

Subject Students on Work Experience – Caps

H Attached is a tear/off slip which should be completed prior to the Christmas break. for

NP the student working in yr dept. [The completed form should be returned to my office.

— — — — — — — — — — — — — — ✂

MAKEPEACE AND STANDING LTD

Report on Work Experience – u/score

Name of Student ..............................

Week Ending ..............................

Dept ..............................

Supervisor ..............................

Attendance (please tick or cross each day, for am/pm)

| Day | am | pm | Duties |
|---|---|---|---|
| Monday | .... | ...... | ...... |
| Tuesday | .... | | |
| Wed. | | | |
| Thurs. | | | |
| Friday. | | | |

Double Spacing

**No. 16** Type the following invoice.

Invoice No. 016775 dated 30 March 1988
to The Principal
Sasha Secretarial College
d. 95 Thames ~~Street~~ St
WOOLWICH WL9 6AR
VAT Reg No is 234 5932 44
Under Description put:

| | |
|---|---|
| lc Workshop Repairs to | Total |
| Adler 131D typewriter S/N 41074498 | 32.50 |
| " " " " 313883 | 87.50 |
| Olivetti daisy wheels | 35.00 |
| Callout charges to repair | |
| lc 54 Typewriters @ £6 each | 324.00 |
| 1 " @ £13.50 | 13.50 |
| Total | 492.50 |
| + VAT @ 15% | 73.80 |
| NET TOTAL | 566.30 |

**No. 17** Please type this letter plus a carbon copy on suitably sized paper.

Ref 23/3 dated 14/9/88 to Miss Linda Browne
18 PRATTS LANE Wimbledon SW19 4TW

Dear Miss B

Thank you for returning the form enclosed with my letter of June 1988; I now write to invite you to
uc attend the One Day conference for new examiners which will be held at

Central Hall, Westminster, London SW1.
on Wednesday 17/10/88

For the greater part of the day delegates will be divided into seminar groups and a detailed programme together with details of the groups is enclosed with this letter.

The Conference begins with registration and coffee between 10.00 and 10.30. There will be a break for lunch from 12.30 to 13.30 and the day will end at approx ~~about~~ 16.30 hours.

We look forward to welcoming you to the group of examiners attached to our Board. Should you have any
uc queries regarding the conference please contact me on extension 6500 at the above number.

Yours sincerely

Gill Sugden

Conference organizer

**No. 18** This is a circular letter which will fit onto A5 paper.

Date : 16/12/87

Dear member

⌊in full The AGM of the LOXLEY Resident's ASSOC

l.c. will be held at the YMCA, Hailsham Room, on

Sunday, 16/1/88 at 7.30 pm.

Programme for the Evening

7.30 Report from Chairman

8.00 Election of Committee followed by AOB

8.30. Talk by Councillor Smith on ⌊ the

⌊plans for main A46 Road in 1989.

9.00 Drinks, coffee, + light refreshments [will be available]

in the area of the main bar

I look forward to seeing you at the

meeting.

Yours sinc.

Reginald Walker

Chairman.

**No. 19** Display the following notice, putting the items in ascending price order.

Centre + UC

Auf Wiedersehen Wine Co

Wine Tasting Evening

| | | | |
|---|---|---|---|
| 39774 | 1982 | Liebfraumilch | £ 2.75 |
| 80861 | 1981 | Detzemer Maximer Dry Red | £ 3.75 |
| 33221 | 1983 | Walsheimer Bischofskreuz (BISCHOFSKREUZ) | £ 3.99 |
| 32222 | 1980 | Kallstatter Feuerberg | £ 4.29 |
| 36789 | 1983 | Nussdorfer Freiburg Dry | £ 3.75 |
| 90999 | 1982 | Rauenthaler Steinmecher | £ 4.49 |
| 34999 | 1983 | Woellsteiner Rheingrafenstein | £5.99 |
| 30566 | 1980 | Ersckhalma Bischofsberg | £ 4.59. |

VAT at 15% is not included in the above prices

A discount is available on a case of 18 bottles

× × × × × × ×

**No. 20** Type the following set of names and addresses either on envelopes or sheets of A4 paper folded into A6 size. Remember that letters after a person's name do not have a full stop.

Mrs A White JP
36 Victoria Row
St Albans Herts AL9 6HT

Dr Daphne Green
9 Cross Street MISSISSAUGA Ontario CANADA

Rev Peter Robertson
The Rectory
WOLDINGHAM SURREY WD2 6JE

Prof M. Evans MSc BA MBIM
86 Circle Gardens
London SW15 8PT

Maj J/S Seathwaite VC, DSO,
The Maltings
Wigan Lancs
WG3 4LA

for the attention of James McTavish (mark private & confidential)
Castle-Estate Agents
101 Fulham Road
London SW6 4QR

cont.

The principal
Sasha Secretarial College
95 Thames Street
WOOLWICH WL9 6AR

Gardeners' World
BBC Radio 4 PO Box 22
Bristol B99 8AB

Mr + Mrs S Smith
Apt 208 97 Aranui Road
Auckland NZ

## Keys to Exercises

### No. 1

It seems to have become the vogue to build replicas of boats used on voyages of discovery several hundred years ago, and then to try to sail them along the same routes to their original destinations.

The latest attempt to re-enact such a voyage is with a replica of 'The Golden Hind' - the boat Sir Francis Drake sailed to St Thomas in the Virgin Islands.

However, after only 24 hours, the ship had run aground on a mudbank at the mouth of the River Avon, and the ship's cat had deserted! No further problems were anticipated on the 7-week voyage once she had been refloated and had sailed away.

Check that you have correct line spacing between paragraphs. Check also that you have no mixed figures and words and that you have as straight a right-hand margin as possible.

### No. 2

It is really difficult to make up your mind when you want to buy a Microcomputer. There are a bewildering number of points to be considered. The first of these is whether you need a computer at all and what you will use it for. Once you have established a need, do you choose the hardware or the software? Apparently, the latter.

When you know what you want to do on the machine you look for the software that best suits these needs and that you find most 'user-friendly'. Having made that decision you then look for the hardware on which to run the programs. Don't think that ends the decision-making, however, because you will probably also need a printer - the choice is usually between dot-matrix, NLQ (near letter quality), daisywheel or thermal, depending on the speed and quality you require.

What about the price? Probably the best idea is to have an upper limit in mind and to discount software, machinery and printers which exceed this amount as you go through the various stages of making up your mind.

**No. 3**

MAKING CORRECTIONS

Some attempt has been made to estimate the ease of correcting mistakes in text when the typist does not have a self-correcting element on the keyboard. Factors which need to be considered with fluids are the ease of application, how well the mistake is covered, how quickly the product dries, and the ease with which one can type over the correction. There is also the problem with a liquid of how quickly it thickens. Some makes seem to thicken up rapidly and as most of them come in narrow-necked bottles, they get 'gunged' up and the brush won't come out easily. Over a period of time the resulting waste can become quite costly.

Coated paper strips are less messy and can be bought either in a colour to match the paper being used or as a plastic film for use with carbon ribbons.

Both fluid and coated paper are useful depending on the type of correction being made and its position on the paper. Still, for ease of use, and speed, the coated paper strips are probably the most popular as well as the cheapest method to use.

With a handwritten passage you can assume that the typed text will take approximately ⅔ the amount of space. Therefore, in this passage, margins of 1½ in would have been suitable and a top margin of 1½ in, i.e. turn up 10 lines.

**No. 4**

P A V E W E L L
L A N D S C A P E S

TARMACKING

Crazy Paving

ORNAMENTAL WALLS

Stone Fireplaces

GRASS CUTTING

Tree Lopping

X X X X X X X X

We are a reliable company and can
GUARANTEE our clients a

F I R S T  C L A S S  J O B !

X X X X X X X X

ESTIMATES FREE

121 London Road
EPSOM
Surrey

PHONE TODAY

X X X X X X X X

## No. 5

SOME TOWNS

| | | | |
|---|---|---|---|
| Alton | Birmingham | Rotherham | Salford |
| Alnwick | Belfast | Rochester | Southampton |
| Accrington | Bradford | Rotherhithe | Sunderland |
| Ashford | Bournemouth | Runcorn | Swansea |
| Appledore | Barnstaple | Ripon | Salisbury |

## No. 6

CROSS-CHANNEL PASSENGER TRAFFIC

(in million passengers pa)

| | 1980 Actual | 2000 Projection | % growth pa 1980 - 2000 |
|---|---|---|---|
| Total Foot Passengers | 9.0 | 19.4 | 3.9 |
| Total Sea Passengers | 18.2 | 44.9 | 4.6 |
| Air Passengers | 2.4 | 3.5 | 1.9 |
| TOTAL PASSENGERS* | 20.6 | 48.4 | 4.4 |

Total cross-Channel passenger traffic to Belgium grew by nearly 3% pa between 1970 and 1980.

## No. 7

DIVISION OF WORDS

| | | |
|---|---|---|
| procedure<br>satisfaction<br>relevant<br>friendship | complacent<br>preference<br>government<br>examination | atmosphere<br>agriculture<br>recognition<br>typewriter |

All these words can easily be divided if they come towards the end of a line of typing.

## No. 8

SCHEDULE OF TRAVELLING TIME

| | Total Time | | Walking/Waiting Time | |
|---|---|---|---|---|
| | hrs | mins | hrs | mins |
| London Paris air | 4 | 25 | 1 | 45 |
| " " sea | 7 | 25 | 1 | 10 |
| London Brussels air | 4 | 00 | 1 | 45 |
| " " sea | 7 | 45 | 1 | 10 |

## No. 9

JOB CREATION - THE CHANNEL FIXED LINK

| Employment Type | Employment Created | |
|---|---|---|
| | Direct | Indirect |
| Construction Workers | 800 - 1 000 | 1 200 - 1 500 |
| Electricians | 2 000 - 3 000 | 2 600 - 4 000 |
| Carpenters and Joiners | 3 500 - 5 000 | 6 000 - 8 000 |

## No.10

WOMEN MANAGERS AS A PERCENTAGE OF TOTAL - 1979

| Managerial Group | % Managers who are women |
|---|---|
| General Management | Not available |
| Managerial | |
| Production, works and maintenance | 20.3 |
| Managers and Works Foremen | 4.6 |
| Site and other Managers | 2.9 |
| Transport Managers | 3.4 |
| Managers in warehousing and materials handling | 2.7 |
| Office Managers | 19.1 |
| Managers in wholesale and retail distribution | 30.4 |
| Publicans, Restaurateurs and Club Stewards | 41.6 |
| All Managers, but excluding those in offices | |
| Wholesale and retail distribution, Publicans, Restaurateurs and Club Stewards | 10.1 |

Source EC Labour Force Survey 1979

**No. 11**

Our Ref  JB/CA19

1 November 1988

Mrs J Blythe
80 Langley Road
BERKHAMPSTEAD  Herts
BK6 HE7

Dear Mrs Blythe

Account Number  19860437

I am writing in reply to your letter of last Thursday to inform you that we have paid the 2 cheques for £387 and £550 into your above-named account.  We have, at the same time, transferred £1 000 to your deposit account as requested.  The balance remaining on your current account as at close of business yesterday was £842.

Yours sincerely
BERKHAMPSTEAD BANK

John Smiley
MANAGER

## No. 12

Our Ref  RR/85RW

2 November 1988

R Reardon Esq
97 London Road
BLACKHEATH
London  SE3 6BL

Dear Mr Reardon

I have pleasure in writing with final details of the arrangements we have made for you, your wife, and your 2 children Elizabeth and Heather.

| | | |
|---|---|---|
| 1 | 19 June 1986 | Heathrow to Singapore |
| | 29 June 1986 | Onward flight Singapore to Hong Kong |
| | 4 July 1986 | Onward flight Hong Kong to Kathmandu |
| | 9 July 1986 | Return flight Kathmandu to Heathrow, London |

2 Hotel accommodation of 2 double rooms each with private bath at

Luxor Palace, Singapore

Holiday Inn, Hong Kong

Imperial Palace Hotel, Kathmandu

3 Arrangements with Asiacar for a small self-drive car to be waiting at the hotels in Singapore and Hong Kong on your arrival.  Keys will be at reception.

4 I enclose details of the various excursions and short walking tours that can be made from Kathmandu.  Should any be of interest to you it may be possible to make reservations prior to your departure.

5 I also enclose particulars of the 2 personal/medical/baggage insurance schemes we offer.  When you have decided on the one you wish to take out for you and your family perhaps you will return the completed Proposal Form to me.

I hope these arrangements meet with your wishes, and look forward to hearing from you shortly.

Yours sincerely
FAR EAST TRAVEL CO

James Browne
Personal Tours Manager

## No. 13

M E M O R A N D U M

FROM Accounts Department DATE 9 March 1988

TO Sales Manager REF AD/GS

SUBJECT Jameson Brothers

Would you please note that the above account holders have exceeded their credit limit. We have made some investigations and understand that the company are in some financial difficulty. Therefore, no further orders should be accepted from them until their account is brought back within the limit as set.

Would you please see that all members of your sales staff receive this information.

cc Managing Director
Marketing Manager

## No. 14

M E M O R A N D U M

FROM Dean's Secretary DATE 15 July 1988

TO All members of staff REF DS/GS

SUBJECT Retirement of Porter

I am sure that by now you know that the Porter George Travolta is retiring at the end of this term after being with the College for almost 15 years.

Anyone who would like to contribute to a leaving present for George is asked to bring their money to my office before 20 July. There will be a presentation by the Dean at the end of term staff meeting on 21st July.

**No. 15**

FROM Personnel Manager                DATE 15 December 1987

TO All Departmental Heads                REF PM/GS

SUBJECT STUDENTS ON WORK EXPERIENCE

Attached is a tear-off slip which should be completed prior to the Christmas break for the student working in your department.

The completed form should be returned to my office.

---

MAKEPEACE AND STANDING LTD

Report on Work Experience

Name of Student ..............................................

Week ending ..................................................

Department ...................................................

Supervisor ...................................................

Attendance (please tick or cross each day for am and pm)

| Day | am | pm | Duties |
|---|---|---|---|
| Monday | ... | ... | ........................................ |
| Tuesday | ... | ... | ........................................ |
| Wednesday | ... | ... | ........................................ |
| Thursday | ... | ... | ........................................ |
| Friday | ... | ... | ........................................ |

**No. 16**

INVOICE

Number 016775

30 March 1984

The Principal
Sasha Secretarial College
95 Thames Street
Woolwich WL9 6AR

VAT REGISTRATION NO 234 5932 44

| QUANTITY | DESCRIPTION | UNIT COST | TOTAL | |
|---|---|---|---|---|
| | Workshop repairs to | | | |
| | Adler 131D typewriter S/N 41074498 | | 32.50 | |
| | Adler 131D typewriter S/N 313883 | | 87.50 | |
| | Olivetti daisy wheels | | 35.00 | |
| | Callout charges to repair | | | |
| | 54 typewriters @ £6.00 each | 6.00 | 324.00 | |
| | 1 typewriter @ £13.50 | 13.50 | 13.50 | |
| | TOTAL | | 492.50 | |
| | - VAT @ 15% | | 73.80 | |
| | NET TOTAL | | 566.30 | |

**No. 17**

Ref 23/3

14 September 1988

Miss Linda Browne
18 Pratts Lane
Wimbledon SW19 4TW

Dear Miss Browne

Thank you for returning the form enclosed with my letter of June 1988; I now write to invite you to attend the One Day Conference for new examiners which will be held at

Central Hall, Westminster, London SW1

on Wednesday 17 October 1988.

The Conference begins with registration and coffee between 10.00 and 10.30. There will be a break for lunch from 12.30 to 13.30 and the day will end at approximately 16.30 hours.

For the greater part of the day delegates will be divided into seminar groups and a detailed programme together with details of the groups is enclosed with this letter.

We look forward to welcoming you to the group of examiners attached to our Board. Should you have any queries regarding the Conference please contact me on extension 6500 at the above number.

Yours sincerely

Gill Sugden
Conference Organizer

Enc

## No. 18

16 December 1987

Dear Member

The Annual General Meeting of the Loxley Residents' Association will be held at the YMCA, Hailsham Road, on Sunday 16 January 1988, at 7.30pm.

Programme for the Evening

| | |
|---|---|
| 7.30 | Report for the Chairman |
| 8.00 | Election of the Committee followed by Any Other Business |
| 8.30 | Talk by Councillor Smith on plans for the main A46 road in 1989 |
| 9.00 | Drinks, coffee and light refreshments will be available in one area of the main bar |

I look forward to seeing you at the meeting.

Yours sincerely

Reginald Walker
Chairman

**No. 19**

AUF WIEDERSEHEN WINE COMPANY

Wine Tasting Evening

| | | | |
|---|---|---|---|
| 39774 | 1982 | Liebfraumilch | £2.75 |
| 36789 | 1983 | Nussdorfer Freiberg Dry | £3.75 |
| 33221 | 1983 | Walsheimer Bischofskreuz | £3.99 |
| 32222 | 1980 | Kallstatter Feuerberg | £4.29 |
| 90999 | 1982 | Rauenthaler Steinmecher | £4.49 |
| 30566 | 1980 | Ersekhaima Bischofsberg | £4.59 |
| 34999 | 1983 | Woellsteiner Rheingrafenstein | £5.99 |
| 80861 | 1981 | Detzemer Maximer Dry Red | £8.75 |

VAT at 15% is not included in the above prices

A discount is available on a case of 18 bottles

o o o o o o o o o o

**No.20**

Mrs A White JP
36 Victoria Row
ST ALBANS Herts
AL9 6HT

Gardeners' World
BBC Radio 4
PO Box 22
BRISTOL B99 8AB

Dr Daphne Green
9 Cross Street
MISSISSAUGA Ontario
CANADA

Mr and Mrs S Smith
Apt 208
97 Aranui Road
AUCKLAND New Zealand

The Very Rev Peter Robertson
The Rectory
WOLDINGHAM Surrey
WD2 6JE

Prof M Evans MSc BA MBIM
86 Circle Gardens
London SW15 8PT

Maj S Seathwaite VC DSO
The Maltings
WIGAN Lancs
WG3 4LA

PRIVATE & CONFIDENTIAL

For the attention of James McTavish Esq

Castle - Estate Agents
101 Fulham Road
LONDON SW6 4QR

The Principal
Sasha Secretarial College
95 Thames Street
WOOLWICH WL9 6AR